The Hidden Organic Remedy:

Nature as Higher Power

Michael J. Cohen, Ph.D.

This workbook consists of a detailed immersion into the accredited Organic Psychology methods and materials that were applied in Mike Cohen's and Stephen MacKay's special "Nature as Higher Power" addiction recovery workshop, June 2013. The book and its associated course introduces Cohen's multi-sensory process of Educating, Counseling and Healing with Nature. The art of its empirical science is a guaranteed pure, therapy, recovery and spirituality tool. Anybody may benefit by using its sensory contacts with natural areas as a part of their personal or professional growth and livelihood.

Organic Psychology - Natural Attraction Ecology – Applied Ecopsychology

The Natural Systems Thinking Process

Project NatureConnect

Project NatureConnect

Institute of Applied Ecopsychology, Akamai University

Educating, Counseling and Healing With Nature

Accredited Courses, Degrees, Workshops, Grants, Books

Institute of Global Education

Box 1605, Friday Harbor, WA 98250

360-378-6313

Email: nature@interisland.net

www.ecopsych.com

Dedicated to David Suzuki because I believe he values this book far more than he knows.

History and Acknowledgements

Thanks is given to Steven MacKay, MPCP, RCS, RPC, who suggested that a workshop be offered to his 12-step clients that would present and Warranty facts that validate the art of Educating, Counseling and Healing With Nature (ECHN) and its Organic Psychology science of Natural Attraction Ecology. This opportunity motivated me to present ECHN as an Avatar of Planet Earth and help qualified others do likewise as described in this book and the Warranty that developed. My appreciation is also given to the volunteer faculty who help coordinate the core of the Project NatureConnect program, Theresa Sweeney, Leslie Whitcomb, Stacey Mallory, SaVonni Yestanti, Donna Elston and Pamela Hoke along with those who have confirmed the Warranty and the many others who help sustain Project NatureConnect.

I recommend the books "Eco-Art Therapy - Creative Activities That Let Earth Teach" by Theresa Sweeney and "Natural Self Discovery" by Pamela Hoke to further "Nature as Higher Power."

TABLE OF CONTENTS

PREFACE

Nature, including humanity, can be seen as an attractive dance of the eons that has the ability to produce optimums of life, diversity, peace, fairness and cooperation throughout the Web of Life. Nature's sanely organizes, corrects, heals and balances itself and the Web without producing our garbage, pollution or unwarranted abusiveness.

We are part of Nature but our central thinking and feeling in Industrial Society is, on average, over ninety-nine percent of the time disconnected from Nature's dance in natural areas. Over ninety-five percent of our physical presence is indoors. For this reason, what and how we think and feel during a captivating period in an attractive natural area helps us discover, experience and express our natural self, the unadulterated root and truth of our being.

We suffer our disorders because our excessively nature-separated lives prevent us from experiencing authentic Nature's way and its joy even though we are it. Because of this hurtful but "normal" loss to our body mind and spirit we each suffer destructive addictions to things that take away the disconnection pain. We want; we feel there is never enough and this makes Nature appear to be the enemy we must conquer or exploit to gain its fulfilling resources.

Devoid of Nature's healing and balancing ways, our mentality is not whole. We are seldom able to solve the personal, social and environmental problems that result from the undeclared but obvious war against Nature that we learn to fight in and around us. Sadly, we deny this war and its effects by calling it part of of "progress" "excellence" or "economic growth."

This book's Education Counseling and Healing with Nature (ECHN) activity connections enable us consciously to be the dance of nature that we were born. It engages us in Nature's love and intelligence. For decades this process has been an additional souce of information and knowing for any individual as well as a too often ignored source of higher power in recovery programs (5). ECHN gives us the ability to reverse and prevent excessive disconnection from, and prejudice against Nature's dance within and about us. The "inconvenient truths" of ECHN help us make unparalleled contributions to personal, social and global well-being.

Due to our excessive separation of our psyche from nature's purifying and self-correcting energies we have become in too many ways an environmentally and socially corrupt society. This often means that our commonly issued assurances are also corrupt. For this reason, as notarized in Appendix A, *Nature as Higher Power* (NHP) is certified organic. I warranty that those who love nature or truly care about the well-being of individuals, communities and natural areas will improve their personal and professional life. This happens because, using Nature as a resource or form of higher power in natural areas they benefit from unadulterated sensory contact with the reality of Nature's beauty, healing and purifying energies, in and around them.

The art-science-spirit process of NHP helps us produce what's missing: whole-mind, Earth connected truth and happiness accompanied by beneficial rather than adverse side effects. Because NHP recognizes that sensations and feelings are legitimate natural facts of life, it is an attractive remedy for problem solving, including addiction challenges, a means for self-improvement that is just as honest and valuable as sunshine.

For those who see that we live in and benefit from the scientifically defined Standard Universe of today, NHP provides far greater wisdom, joy and support than we get from corruption in our leadership and institutions. Bewildered (wilderness separated), the latter have misguided us in many ways to create the troubles that we suffer and seldom remedy. *Nature as Higher Power* gives us a readily available therapy and/or livelihood that enables us to resolve this dilemma as we add it to our personal and professional life.

INTRODUCTION

The beneficial "miracles" performed by science and technology for the advancement of the human condition deserves our applause for a job well done. The success and daily progress of today's artificial way of life is amazing, something never before been seen on Earth. On one hand, its scientific process deserves our great thanks for the wonderful benefits and the well-being it has created on many levels. On the other hand, our artificial ways have become excessively disconnected from Nature and its dance in and around us. The corruption, destruction and suffering produced by the "side effects" of Nature's absence in our lives must also be acknowledged, no less harnessed.

For two thousand years profound thoughts and feelings have identified our nagging personal and global side-effect problems. Wonderful ideas have been offered as solutions for them. What has been missing is a practical process to implement our best thinking, *a tool that enables us to do what we know is reasonable and necessary to do.* This tool must be a trustable antidote for our nature-disconnected mentality and relationships if we are to increase personal, social and environmental well-being. *Nature as Higher Power* (NHP) offers a major remedy in this regard. It is an easily applicable social technology that gives us the means to address the heart of what ails us.

At this late date our society has yet to identify the underlying source of our corrupt ways, no less engage in an effective process that corrects it. The dysfunctions and disorders that accompany our great achievements indicate that, unlike nature itself, we have a monumental short circuit in the way Industrial Society works. We demean or have lost subjective contact with nature's wisdom and are becoming more and more addicted to more advanced artificial means we invent to replace it, *and they can't.* With respect to nature and the life of its eons of harmonic balance and beauty, we know of no substitute for the real thing.

Like all species, we were born with the biological ability to love and live in balance with the purity, wellness and integrity of Earth. The destructive, nature-disconnected warp in how we think and feel has separated our mentality from the organics of the natural world. It has unbalanced our planet and us to the point that, being biologically identical, we are both at risk. It is as if our misguided mentality has placed a Toyota computer in a Chevrolet.

A corrupt mind is a terrible thing to waste so we don't. Instead we profit from the crooked, unbalanced ways our socialization (indoctrination) has instilled in our outlook. We also profit from selling questionable remedies for the hurtful personal, social and environmental dilemmas that our corrupt thinking causes. In addition, we suppress a practical organic remedy for Industrial Society's exploitation of our body, mind and spirit so as not to impede the unethical profiteering in our economic growth. As Upton Sinclair observed :

> "It is difficult to get people to understand something when their salary (or other reward) depends upon them not understanding it."

We seldom recognize that individually and collectively Industrial Society practices identity theft on a global level. It has legalized its embezzlement of our inborn self, our naturally pure and balanced genetic wholesomeness, under a distorted banner of freedom. This banner is unfair. It does not equally distribute or give the happiness that we gain from nature's balancing and purifying ways any legal or moral rights, no matter the depressing disorders, pain and destruction that this omission produces.

The use of corrupt facts rather than scientifically valid sensory information is the heart of our dilemmas as well as the heart of our inability to stop them. For this reason, *Nature as Higher Power* (NHP) comes with my written Warranty (*Appendix A*) that unequivocally identifies organic information in the book and ECHN that is not adulterated. It strongly suggests that organic NHP processes and information *be reasonably integrated with* any other information, relationship or belief system to reverse our dilemmas.

NHP is only for folks who know that they live in the science-based Standard Universe of the Big Bang and want to learn how to obtain help from and for its ways. We suffer our disorders because many of us physically live in the organics of our Standard Universe but we have learned to think and act from the disasterous false or imaginary fables of unreal places and relationships. This is like fueling a standard automobile with water instead of gasoline; it produces many problems.

The model that this book offers is based on empirical, self-evident facts that demonstrate the validity of its process. It does this under the most challenging circumstances, at a workshop with incarcerated, substance-addicted individuals in a correctional institution. However, because we are bonded and addicted to our out of balance way of life, it also helps any caring person learn how to relate in ways that increase personal, social and environmental well-being in most situations. It guarantees that its information is organic reality, free of corruption, more true and dependable than knowing that the tide will rise and fall. It provides critical preventative and restorative assistance when used most anywhere at any time.

My advanced study of natural areas, while living most of my life in them, qualifies me to issue my Warranty. Without drugs, alcohol or destructive excessiveness, I and others have successfully learned to think, feel and relate based on genuinely connecting with the way that nature works as well as teaching others to accomplish this. After all, it is no scientific secret that, until proven otherwise, everything in nature's perfection is non-literate except humanity, everything is attracted or attached to everything else and is continuously cycling, recycling, changing and purifying so and garbage and pollution are not produced. It is common knowledge that the sun rises and sets and rises again, that Planet Earth is round and acts like or is a living organism that gravity holds us to the planet and like the crest of a wave everything only exists and changes in the immediate moment. We know that micro relationships appear different than macro relationships; that we inherently can learn and relate to the world with more than 5 senses, that air is breathable, water is drinkable, flowers are colorful and the unclouded daytime sky is blue. Yet, at this late date we challenge or disregard these organic truths, rather than embrace and depend upon them as a source of higher power or fundamentals for our socialization. This demonstrates just how fraudulent our thoughts, feelings and relationships have become. Their adulteration has robbed us of the beneficial roots of our being.

We are in trouble because our social foundations are warped-thinking stories yet they direct our technologies and education. By omitting nature's guiding sensory energies from our science, education, relationships and spirituality, the way we administer our complex, high-tech society is like having a goat operate the control tower at O'Hare International Airport.

We habitually learn to think and feel in conjunction with our excessive nature-disconnected and artificial stories and techniques that produce the side-effect problems that we suffer as well as produce our inability to solve them. We even go so far as to question using nature's truths as our higher power no less as a valid sensory source of information and guidance. This is like the belief that drinking whiskey to forget our stressful troubles will cure our alcoholism. We have become addicted to disconnecting from nature and to our nature-disconnected leaders along with the nature-replacement artifacts that they sell us.

NHP enables you to make more complete sense:

> - It empowers you to actively validate and put to work pure organic relationships and knowledge that it helps you discover while you help others do the same.

- It provides a fair, no nonsense way to connect with the drug-free happiness and wisdom of higher power in Nature, Spirit and the Divine.

- It gives you the means to make happen now what our socialization has long ignored, as shown by the quotes and their dates through the ages that NHP includes.

The process the book offers also integrates seamlessly with God beliefs that you may hold. You may choose, as an extension of them, to be a Pantheist (Einstein, Thoreau, Lao Tzu, Sitting Bull, Emerson, Lincoln, Whitman, Chief Seattle, Beethoven and Pete Seeger were Pantheists). NHP empowers you with a tool to organically do what has yet to be done, to act reasonably from classic observations like:

"I believe in God, only I spell it Nature." - **Frank Lloyd Wright circa 1932**

"For what else is Nature but God and the Divine Reason that pervades the whole universe and all its parts." - **Seneca the Younger circa 25 A.D.**

I have designed this book as a hands-on means for a leader or parent to introduce the joy available by using its powerful natural antidote that reverses disorders and addictions (18). The process works best if the leader is already trained to be literate and comfortable knowing that they and earth/nature are one, that Earth is their other body. This enables them to personally share the wisdom they have gained from dealing with past trespasses against their other body, Earth, in and around them.

Sadly, our male dominated history makes classic quotes from males readily available for making a point. Similar quotes are no doubt available from women and I urge women to send them to me so I may include them in later editions.

Organized as a workbook and free course, NHP is extra effective because it provides Activity Page space for immediate notes, questions, activities and drawings, accompany the text that motivates you to produce them. In addition, a handy Personal Value Index is located at the bottom of each text page to help you locate strengths or other areas that you find helpful on it. You may do these pages later to determine the growth or change that has taken place.

The text is in the form of a recent workshop that introduces a long-term Organic Psychology program and that includes the reader as a participant in the workshop. Leader, reader and participant are on equal terms. All pull together as an educational expedition whose purpose is to gain the wonderful feelings and wellness that arise as we come into balance. This produces a high-energy ecstasy of unity that overcomes resistance to this important process.

NHP works because it enables you to enlist nature's healing and purifying powers along with their bliss as your ally all the time. In addition, it helps you continue with an online Educating, Counseling and Healing with Nature (ECHN) program for further improvement or training and grants that can lead to an academic degree or professional certification as a practitioner (www.ecopsych.com). You can become an expert in how to reconnect with nature. The world will surely turn to you for personal and professional assistance as the hurtful effects of our disconnection continue to take their economic and environmental toll. This nature-connection advantage is already working for ECHN students.

The book's NHP workshop is accredited and offered for special on-site leadership training with Dr. Cohen and others on San Juan Island, Washington and elsewhere, by appointment (360.378.6313). The Orientation Course is often a prerequisite for leadership training (http://www.ecopsych.com/orient.html).

NHP can be a companion volume to *Natural Self Discovery* by Pamela Hoke. It is modeled after, and can be offered successfully as a one-day introductory program by presenters who are familiar with its material and who openly share their life-experiences as their personal truths. Otherwise, it takes longer for the process of validating its facts.

Fact by fact, references to easily accessible Internet pages for further information are numbered in the text as well as on an associated work page in *Appendix G.*

NHP is based on the results of research that provides additional information at:
Cohen, M. J. 2008, *Educating Counseling and Healing With Nature* Illumina Publishing.
http://www.ecopsych.com/ksanity.html

Project NatureConnect: *The Miracle of Something from Nothing*
http://www.ecopsych.com/journalessence.html

Project NatureConnect: *PNC Warranty: Singularity in Action*
http://www.ecopsych.com/journalwarranty.html

Project NatureConnect 2007, *Natural Attraction Ecology*
http://www.naturalattractionecology.com

Project NatureConnect: *Nature Connected Health and Wellness Research*
http://www.ecopsych.com/survey.html

Project NatureConnect: The Organic Psychology of Global Citizenship books

"The Web of Life Imperative" "Reconnecting With Nature" ECHN Orientation Course:
http://www.ecopsych.com/orient.html

The process of Educating Counseling and Healing with Nature (ECHN) empowers you to act from these classic observations:

> "We are dysfunctional socially and environmentally because we are cut off and isolated from the world of nature and the natural." - **Albert Gore 1989**

> "I believe that the universe is the manifestation of its attraction to be and to grow, that all its parts are different growths and expressions of the same original attraction. They are all in attractive communication with each other and, thereby, parts of one organic whole. The whole has designed itself in humanity to register in at least fifty-four natural attraction senses. All parts of the whole are so beautiful, and are felt by me so intensely, that I am compelled to love it and to think of it as divine."
> - **Robinson Jeffers circa 1950, extended.**

SPECIAL NOTICE

The key to obtaining the most that you can from this book and its warranty is to apply the suggestions on the Activity Page to attractive information offered in the text. A light grey underline identifies specific activity sections of the text.

CHAPTER 1

PERSONAL EXPERIENCE IS PERSONAL TRUTH

PERSONAL EXPERIENCE IS PERSONAL TRUTH

10:05 AM. "Hi, my name is Mike," is all I said to the 35 drug and alcohol addiction felons in the room at the Correctional Services recovery center. They were there because a Judge had sentenced them to a special organic substance abuse program that includes the art and science of Project NatureConnect's Education, Counseling and Healing with Nature process (ECHN 1, 3). Uniquely, I was teaching them how to create phenomenal sensory moments that let Nature teach as part of their 12-step recovery programs as these moments do in many other programs.

The purpose of my visit was to help this recovery facility discover the value of learning how to use genuine sensory contact with nature as a source of higher power in its variety of 12 step programs. The results were spectacular, environmentally sound and far-reaching for these incarcerated First Nation, Native American and European-Origin participants alike.

In this book I share with you exactly what we did in a one-day workshop and its effects so you, too, may obtain, and help others enjoy its momentous benefits. The program had already proven itself many times over with groups and individuals who were not in jail (5).

Some parts of what we did are not a pretty picture, but that's why they worked. The effects of the picture that Industrial Society paints for itself and each of us are seldom pretty when they are not organic. The outrage over these corrupt and limiting outcomes was the extra energy that motivated exceptional growth in our program participants.

APPLY PRACTICAL FACTS

I said to the group: "I warranty (*Appendix A)* that my purpose in being here is to help your Counselor, Steve, collect and apply practical facts about our relationship with nature. He's learning how to get exceptional results from applying nature's healing and purifying powers to our daily lives. Steve is going to school to master this process and obtain certification and a degree in it. Today you can learn how to do it with him. In fact, as you know, he was once in your situation with drugs and prison." With various shades of enthusiasm the addicts

ACTIVITY PAGE

RESPONSES write your Validations in the space provided below.

RECORD NOTES, Reactions, Questions, Comments, Drawings, Rubs, Samples

INCREASE AWARENESS Write responses to the activities found in Appendix H

DO POWER ACTIVITIES **Match – Resonate – Appreciate – Trust – Celebrate** *(see Appendix B)*.

OPTION: arrange an onsite workshop with Dr. Cohen 1-360-378-6313

Text References are listed by number in Appendix G with online links.

LEARN MORE Master ECHN: online orientation course www.ecopsych.com/orient.html

PASS IT ON: Increase your expertise by 75%. Teach NHP to another person.

all agreed to participate, so I continued. "Let's start with what I've already shared with you. What facts can we discover from me telling you that my name is Mike?"

No answer.

"Is there anybody here that can't hear my voice?" I said.

No response.

"That's good. You see, I was testing to see if anybody was going to be deceitful and say that they could not hear me. If they did I would ask them 'If you can't hear me how did you know to answer the question since you don't read lips?' Some laughed. I thought that was a good sign, they were paying attention.

"OK. That you can hear me means that your sense of Hearing is working. There, that's a fact, right? That you can register my voice and respond to it is your personal truth. I know it is true for you because you experienced it. Do you recognize this, too? If so, say it to each other something like 'I know that hearing the sound of his voice is true for you because you experienced it.' " I had them say this a few times so they became comfortable with doing it, and some did. It produced smiles. They experienced a degree of happiness that a moment before was not present. It was a contentment or fulfillment that they obtained in a good way, meaning to the benefit of all, as there were no destructive side effects from it for them or for anyone else. They became a touch more positive, whole, energized and present. They were now my allies as we continued, and doing this was contagious.

I said, "Nobody can take this 'hearing' truth away from you. I can't talk you out of it, the Administrators can't tell you that you can't have it, that it's not allowed. Your mother can't say you don't have it. If God walked into this room, do you think He could convince you

VALUE INDEX My degree of attraction to the information on this page:

1	2	3	4	5	6	7	8	9	10
	None			Moderate			Strong		

IF IMPORTANT, WHY?

Activity Page

RESPONSES write your Validations in the space provided below.

RECORD NOTES, Reactions, Questions, Comments, Drawings, Rubs, Samples

INCREASE AWARENESS Write responses to the activities found in Appendix H

DO POWER ACTIVITIES **Match – Resonate – Appreciate – Trust – Celebrate** *(see Appendix B).*

OPTION: arrange an onsite workshop with Dr. Cohen 1-360-378-6313

Text References are listed by number in Appendix G with online links.

LEARN MORE Master ECHN: online orientation course www.ecopsych.com/orient.html

PASS IT ON: Increase your expertise by 75%. Teach NHP to another person.

that you can't hear my voice right now? You see, your natural sense of being able to register sound is an innate biological and psychological fact. You own it, nature gave it to you and you experience that it works so let's put that fact first on the fact list that Steve is making.

EFFECTS OF INDOCTRINATION

For you to collect accurate facts about the world is vital. You have been indoctrinated with and traumatized by so many misleading facts about yourself and the world that you have ended up addicted and in jail with some of the symptoms of post-traumatic stress because you have experienced it. You got caught by the authorities. The rest of us are caught by excessive stress that injures us and other unseen, innocent people and places on the planet. To remedy this, this program helps you and others find and use truths that you know make sense and engage in them to replace the corrupt facts and situations that mislead you. Just think about this: most of the facts that we believe are wrong. For example, centuries ago false facts said the Earth was the center of the solar system and universe. True facts corrected this error, yet folks that believed them then were "heretics." They were put in jail until these facts were accepted more than 140 years later. That serves to show how the powers of institutions prevent change *(Appendix C)*.

Today, misleading facts pollute and overuse the Earth so we now take 150 percent more resources from it than it can produce or that we can pay for. That's a form of slow death for Earth and us. It disturbs us for our sense of reason knows that this does not make sense, that we are not reasonable in this regard. That observation produces underlying, earth-shaking erosion of our self-esteem and credibility in relating in socially and environmentally just ways that do not unfairly threaten or eliminate lives, species and habitats. After all, who knows how to make and pay for another planet half the size of Earth and hook it up to Earth so they work identically and support each other? That's presently what is needed (18).

It does not make sense to choose to use a corrupt form of higher power whose 'facts' lead us to excessively conquer nature, in and around us, and promote personal and planetary deterioration. That's not organic, it's the opposite, it's toxic and it's depressing as we see and feel Nature dying. Somebody should declare that using corrupt higher power is a sin or at least a punishable crime, right? After all, aren't you are in jail for using or doing something

VALUE INDEX My degree of attraction to the information on this page:

1   2   3   4   5   6   7   8   9   10
None   Moderate   Strong

IF IMPORTANT, WHY?

ACTIVITY PAGE

RESPONSES write your Validations in the space provided below.

RECORD NOTES, Reactions, Questions, Comments, Drawings, Rubs, Samples

INCREASE AWARENESS Write responses to the activities found in Appendix H

DO POWER ACTIVITIES **Match – Resonate – Appreciate – Trust – Celebrate** *(see Appendix B).*

OPTION: arrange an onsite workshop with Dr. Cohen 1-360-378-6313

Text References are listed by number in Appendix G with online links.

LEARN MORE Master ECHN: online orientation course www.ecopsych.com/orient.html

PASS IT ON: Increase your expertise by 75%. Teach NHP to another person.

stupid?" That got another smile.

"Let's continue," I said, "Now, you also can see my hands and lips moving, correct?" Some nodded in agreement. "The ability to register Motion is also a happiness, an undeniable truth for you because it registered directly on your senses, you experienced it, you would not want to lose it, correct? You would lose the joy of watching football or movies, right?" Again they nodded. I had them again repeat with me, "I know my sense of Motion is true for me because I experienced it." I said, "So there's two other facts we have discovered. One is that your sense of Motion is working and it can make you conscious of movement. The second is that that our natural senses are our inherent ability for us to register the real world. We can do that because we experience them. Let's put both those truths on the fact list." Steve did. "Oh," I said, "And those of you who have smiled at parts of what we have been learning because you enjoyed experiencing them demonstrates that you have a sense of humor. Steve, that's a third fact to add to the list."

VALUING

Charley, can you see my hand? 'Yes,' he replied, and I had them all say with me to Charley, "And we know it is true for you because you experienced it." I call this little fact-awareness phrase a "Spoken Self-Evident Truth and Happiness Validation" and I represent it by the word: *Validate*. I use *Validate* in italic here. It signifies that discussion took place and the group, or some of its members spoke the validation for themselves and/or for and with others. What is monumental about this is that we are validating sensation as a fact. The sensation of thirst becomes just as true a fact as is water as a material. *Validate* can take a wide range of time depending upon the degree of familiarity and knowledge in the Leader/Facilitator. Each validation can be augmented and strengthened by adding to it processes described in *Appendix B*. *Validate* is the senses of Reason, Literacy and Consciousness resonating with input from one or more additional senses.

We are all under the destructive influence of our society's corruption. The facilitator's challenge is not to be subject to their personal addictions or values and affect others with them. The task is to let the natural senses "speak" for themselves as unadulterated sensations/

VALUE INDEX My degree of attraction to the information on this page:

1	2	3	4	5	6	7	8	9	10
	None				Moderate			Strong	

IF IMPORTANT, WHY?

ACTIVITY PAGE

RESPONSES write your Validations in the space provided below.

RECORD NOTES, Reactions, Questions, Comments, Drawings, Rubs, Samples

INCREASE AWARENESS Write responses to the activities found in Appendix H

DO POWER ACTIVITIES **Match – Resonate – Appreciate – Trust – Celebrate** *(see Appendix B).*

OPTION: arrange an onsite workshop with Dr. Cohen 1-360-378-6313

Text References are listed by number in Appendix G with online links.

LEARN MORE Master ECHN: online orientation course www.ecopsych.com/orient.html

PASS IT ON: Increase your expertise by 75%. Teach NHP to another person.

sensitivities/sensibilities so we may begin to think like nature works.

NOTE: *You may master the ability to Validate through subsidized Project NatureConnect online courses and training as well as workshops with Dr. Cohen and others on San Juan Island, Washington and elsewhere. By appointment 360.378.6313 <nature@interisland.net>*

Validate is an organic affirmation for scientific thinking and feeling that helps folks strengthen their contact with reality. When I think of *Validate* it's a reasonable and conscious story of the moment, a reminder to do it, to actually say "And I know it is true for (you, me or us) because (you, me or we) experienced it." Taking a few, deep, earth-connecting breaths (21), and then saying this truth for each sensation and fact we discover is a very important habit. It brings experiential knowledge into the immediate conscious, reasoning and literate moment where it becomes a self-evident fact, part of our body, mind and spirit dance. It is a full, first-hand experience way of knowing as natural human beings rather than just as a story. Doing it is a practical, free antidote and preventative for being a victim of destructive falsehoods. It produces happiness and you can strengthen it at will (Appendix B). It's more reasonable, lasting and safer than using detrimental or addictive drugs to do the same thing.

"Now," I said, "I'm going to tell you the very simple but significant secret for getting out of the troubles you are in as well as living in happy ways that prevent their recurrence and help others, too, Ready? Here it is. Always *Validate* each time you discover a fact that is true for you because your senses registered it, because you experienced it. This is simple enough to do; we've already done it a couple of times. Being literate is part of our human wholeness.

We each must put into the literate part of our mind what we know is true for us because words strongly influence how and what we think and feel. They are part of the way our mentality works. If we don't get them right, we end up going wrong.

Ask yourself whether you would rather enjoy your amazing gift of words or would you choose instead to be 'dumb,' meaning you can't talk at all or speak reasonably.

You know that *untrue* words and ideas have misled you. They have landed you in jail as well as addict you and make you suffer the troubles that this causes. For this reason it's vital that

VALUE INDEX My degree of attraction to the information on this page:

1   2   3   4   5   6   7   8   9   10
     None   Moderate   Strong
IF IMPORTANT, WHY?

ACTIVITY PAGE

RESPONSES write your Validations in the space provided below.

RECORD NOTES, Reactions, Questions, Comments, Drawings, Rubs, Samples

INCREASE AWARENESS Write responses to the activities found in Appendix H

DO POWER ACTIVITIES **Match – Resonate – Appreciate – Trust – Celebrate** *(see Appendix B)*.

OPTION: arrange an onsite workshop with Dr. Cohen 1-360-378-6313

Text References are listed by number in Appendix G with online links.

LEARN MORE Master ECHN: online orientation course www.ecopsych.com/orient.html

PASS IT ON: Increase your expertise by 75%. Teach NHP to another person.

you make yourself as aware as possible of what is true for you. You accomplish this mighty feat by Validating, by putting into words and saying aloud, or better still, writing, after each fact you identify 'I know it's true for me because I experienced it.' In addition, you double your learning by doing the same for others here as you help them do it for themselves. If you don't continuously Validate here today you are missing out on making contact with your uncorrupted higher power, with higher power that you know is true for you because your natural senses, unadulterated, experienced it.

Now, take a minute. Think about the facts we have found and validated already and the importance of validating, and if it makes sense and it true for you Validate validating. Say aloud, 'I know validating is true for me because I experienced it.' After that, say it about the others here in the group that you experienced watching them benefit from it, 'I know validating is true for you because I experienced you experiencing it."

We repeated the *Validate* process noting the fact that they were conscious of the senses of Sound, Motion and Humor and that this was accurate for them so our sense of Consciousness was working and that was a fact we must *Validate*. From that point on I insisted that they say in full "And we know it is true for (you, me or us) because (you, I or we) experienced it," whenever a personal fact of life for others or themselves was evident, while Steve wrote these facts down. I'll continually notate this process occurred here with "*Validate.*" It's even more effective if folks write out these validation words because writing exercises many more senses than just speaking. This makes the experience more powerful and supports journaling.

VALIDATING SENSES AND SENSUALITY

I continued by asking the group if they could understand my words and read the writing on the chart hanging on the wall. They responded that they could, so their sense and sensation of Literacy, of registering stories, was a true fact for them. *Validate.* They also recognized that it was sensible for them to acknowledge that it made sense that what they sensed was true for them, and that the words they read also made sense to them. This meant that their sense of making sense of their senses, their sense and sensations of Reason, was yet another true fact for them because they experienced it. *Validate.* They could see various colors so their sense of Color was true for them because they experienced it. *Validate.* They could determine whether things were close or far from them so their sense of Distance was intact. *Validate.* They

ACTIVITY PAGE

RESPONSES write your Validations in the space provided below.

RECORD NOTES, Reactions, Questions, Comments, Drawings, Rubs, Samples

INCREASE AWARENESS Write responses to the activities found in Appendix H

DO POWER ACTIVITIES **Match – Resonate – Appreciate – Trust – Celebrate** *(see Appendix B)*.

OPTION: arrange an onsite workshop with Dr. Cohen 1-360-378-6313

Text References are listed by number in Appendix G with online links.

LEARN MORE Master ECHN: online orientation course www.ecopsych.com/orient.html

PASS IT ON: Increase your expertise by 75%. Teach NHP to another person.

could register Hunger and Thirst so these senses were also undeniable personal and group attributes. *Validate.*

"How many senses have you been taught that you learn from and know the world by?" I asked. They agreed that it was five: Sight, Sound, Taste, Touch and Smell. *Validate.*

I said, "OK, now think about this. We just sensed, acknowledged and occasionally laughed about the fact that we registered undeniable facts, our personal truths, our senses of Sound, Motion, Sight, Consciousness, Literacy, Reason, Color, Distance, Thirst, Hunger and Humor, too. So now let's use what we have discovered and *Validate* it. Now, let's use our sense of Reason to consider this fact: only two of these eleven senses, Sight and Sound are amongst the five we are taught that we are born with and learn from. Doesn't our sense of Reason register and report that this is true, and that we have made a reasonable and correct observation. *Validate.*

Now think about this in addition to what we just validated: we have factually determined the truth that we individually and collectively have an additional nine senses. *Validate.* What does this tell your senses of Reason, Consciousness and Literacy? We have already assured that these three senses are working for us. Do you think the 'We have and learn from 5–senses story' is accurate or is it a corrupt half-truth in that we have experienced many more senses? Our sense of reason signals 'half-truth' and this makes us feel sensible and adequate because we have discovered a falsehood." *Validate*

Educating, Counseling and Healing With Nature (ECHN) empowers you to act from these classic observations:

> "Nothing is more indisputable than our senses."
> - **Jean Le Rond d'Alembert circa 1752**
>
> "The senses, being the explorers of the world, open the way to knowledge."
> - **Maria Montessori circa 1897**

MULTISENSORY KNOWING

ACTIVITY PAGE

RESPONSES write your Validations in the space provided below.

RECORD NOTES, Reactions, Questions, Comments, Drawings, Rubs, Samples

INCREASE AWARENESS Write responses to the activities found in Appendix H

DO POWER ACTIVITIES **Match – Resonate – Appreciate – Trust – Celebrate** *(see Appendix B)*.

OPTION: arrange an onsite workshop with Dr. Cohen 1-360-378-6313

Text References are listed by number in Appendix G with online links.

LEARN MORE Master ECHN: online orientation course www.ecopsych.com/orient.html

PASS IT ON: Increase your expertise by 75%. Teach NHP to another person.

Here's another truth. In my nature-connection model I have found 54 natural senses *(Appendix E)*. Researchers have shown that we genetically inherit each of them. However, we learn to acknowledge only five of them and this pertains directly to you.

You see, you are incarcerated here because like many of us you never learned to make sense of the natural dance of your lives and relationships using the combined intelligence of your 54 natural senses. You mostly thought you only had and used five of them. When you felt stupid or hurt, it was because you were denied your right to know that you were only being taught to reason with ten percent of your inherent 54-sense capacity to think, feel and build good relationships in mutually supportive balance.

We can see from the destructive effects of Industrial Society on the natural environment that it is involved in an undeclared war against nature, around us and in us, too. Our war wounds hurt, we addict to things that temporarily remove the pain, we can't stop and become excessive. As part of its conquest of nature, corruption in Industrial Society misled, hurt and molded your nature, your mind, body and spirit, while you were very young and unaware, as well as today. Now it is punishing you for its error, for its disastrous effects on your self-worth and relationships. You seldom find this happening in nature-centered societies."

At this point, one participant offered that he should have told the Judge that it was the corruption in Industrial Society that was guilty of a crime against him and nature, not him, and others agreed. They also agreed that it was completely their responsibility to recognize and remedy what had happened to them by thoughtfully seeking help. I continued, "That injury, and other similar injuries to your young self, is what urged you to use drugs to tranquilize, or to remove your hurt or your "you are stupid or worthless" story that you learned from the war on nature. You suffer from the same stupidity of the way we injure nature, because you are part of nature. When some types of drugs temporarily tranquilized away your "I am stupid" story they allowed your other 49 senses to safely come into play and gave you the high to enjoy their fulfillment without you being criticized or disciplined. However, this reward also addicted you to the drugs or alcohol and their consequences. To change this situation is like your sense of Reason deciding it's best for you to learn a new language and then actually proceeding to learn it. It's not stupid to recognize that the change takes time as well as takes new skills and repetition to

VALUE INDEX My degree of attraction to the information on this page:

1	2	3	4	5	6	7	8	9	10
	None			Moderate			Strong		

IF IMPORTANT, WHY?

ACTIVITY PAGE

RESPONSES write your Validations in the space provided below.

RECORD NOTES, Reactions, Questions, Comments, Drawings, Rubs, Samples

INCREASE AWARENESS Write responses to the activities found in Appendix H

DO POWER ACTIVITIES **Match – Resonate – Appreciate – Trust – Celebrate** *(see Appendix B).*

OPTION: arrange an onsite workshop with Dr. Cohen 1-360-378-6313

Text References are listed by number in Appendix G with online links.

LEARN MORE Master ECHN: online orientation course www.ecopsych.com/orient.html

PASS IT ON: Increase your expertise by 75%. Teach NHP to another person.

break old habits and find new, more reasonable rewards. Think about this quietly for the next minute, then we'll discuss questions and *Validate* when you recognize its validity."

CORRECTING STUPIDITY

After the minute had passed I repeated, "You are not here because you are stupid and getting into nonsense. You are here because you were misled, you were taught to be this way and you simply got caught while many others didn't so this workshop is not about or for you alone. Most of us are in situations similar to yours. We all disobey the law at some point. The difference is that we were lucky enough not to injure others, or to get apprehended or become addicted to disobeying authority. Think about it. Some examples of common violations that folks enact include: texting while driving a car, or going through stoplights, or over the speed limit; lying on tax forms, lying in general, shoplifting, cheating on exams, jaywalking, driving while drinking, littering, being too rowdy, using false prescriptions or illegal substances, trespassing, personal and environmental abusiveness etc. Each of these is not uncommon and can have unhappy and life-threatening results including jail time. We are all socialized to become crazy-makers; we don't seek help because we have not been caught or punished. Instead, the unknown people places and things we affect are unjustifiably injured or trespassed. We can see our bad effects but our pain and addictions won't let us stop

How about this, how about we stop thinking incorrectly about ourselves right now? Do you remember, think or feel that you have been misled by an injurious or corrupt part of society at home, school or work? Do you think that this has led to you having your present sickness or disorder that you now must remedy? If so, let's put this as a fact on our list because it is true for you, your senses of Reason and Consciousness are experiencing that story right now. Let's share our personal history with each other. *Validate.*

I'm here teaching this nature connection program to Steve and you in order to help you reverse the injurious effects of our Society's misleading education and guidance. It continues in this very moment because the corruption that pervades our society is considered "normal" or unchangeable. On a mass level, this may be so, but you can choose not to be part of it. As I mentioned earlier, what we are facing in using nature as higher power is the same challenge Copernicus faced when the reasonable truths he collected registered on his senses and he

VALUE INDEX My degree of attraction to the information on this page:

1   2   3   4   5   6   7   8   9   10
     None   Moderate   Strong
IF IMPORTANT, WHY?

ACTIVITY PAGE

RESPONSES write your Validations in the space provided below.

RECORD NOTES, Reactions, Questions, Comments, Drawings, Rubs, Samples

INCREASE AWARENESS Write responses to the activities found in Appendix H

DO POWER ACTIVITIES **Match – Resonate – Appreciate – Trust – Celebrate** *(see Appendix B).*

OPTION: arrange an onsite workshop with Dr. Cohen 1-360-378-6313

Text References are listed by number in Appendix G with online links.

LEARN MORE Master ECHN: online orientation course www.ecopsych.com/orient.html

PASS IT ON: Increase your expertise by 75%. Teach NHP to another person.

declared the sun, not the Earth, was the center of the solar system, that the Earth actually moved even though the Bible said that it did not. Even a century later Galileo was placed in jail and house arrest for saying Copernicus was correct. He suffered for our inaccuracy.

You are in jail because the truths that for your welfare your senses signaled to you is that they/ you have been hurt. It's because you used illegal, addictive substances to deal with the hurt that got you into trouble with the law because you trespassed on the legal rights of others to support this 'fix.' Now, you are learning something more reasonable, how to let higher power in nature help you deal with the hurt in a legal, enjoyable and constructive way.

Nature can heal the injuries to your psyche in the same way that it heals a scraped knee. It takes time and sometimes it leaves a scar. Nature sometimes can't change the scar, but in a group such as this one, as you support each other in this work, your supportive, shared thoughts, feelings and experiences become replacements for the scars in each other. In this way you become part of each other's lives as you commune and communicate. You become a true *community* and this brings happiness to your natural sense of Community. This means that each of you holds or is a key for others to connect with 54 natural senses, sensibilities that you and they have in common *(Appendix E)*. The more you do this for each other, the better off you all are. That's why sharing *Validations* is attractive and so important to all."

A MONUMENTAL WARRANTY

What is very different about what I'm teaching you here is that it comes with a Warranty *(Appendix A)*. It guarantees that the key information in my Project NatureConnect (PNC) program is indisputable, organic, felt-sense, scientific fact that is not corrupt and that does not corrupt, until proven otherwise. You can trust it as much as you can trust that the ocean consists of water. It is just like your immediate sensory experiences that we have just explored are true facts for you. They didn't corrupt you or anything else and they were rewarding. That's the opposite of using some of the misguided "facts" that govern Industrial Society.

CORRUPTION

I think we have come to a point where we can validate that it is reasonable and valuable to

VALUE INDEX My degree of attraction to the information on this page:

1	2	3	4	5	6	7	8	9	10
	None			Moderate			Strong		

IF IMPORTANT, WHY?

ACTIVITY PAGE

RESPONSES write your Validations in the space provided below.

RECORD NOTES, Reactions, Questions, Comments, Drawings, Rubs, Samples

INCREASE AWARENESS Write responses to the activities found in Appendix H

DO POWER ACTIVITIES **Match – Resonate – Appreciate – Trust – Celebrate** *(see Appendix B).*

OPTION: arrange an onsite workshop with Dr. Cohen 1-360-378-6313

Text References are listed by number in Appendix G with online links.

LEARN MORE Master ECHN: online orientation course www.ecopsych.com/orient.html

PASS IT ON: Increase your expertise by 75%. Teach NHP to another person.

explore, discover and think with facts that we know are true because we experience them, again like the fact that you can hear the sound of my voice, and not let other influences corrupt this fact. So now let us ask each other this: how much money would it take to have any of you say that you can't hear my voice, or any voice, when you actually can?

Let's say that Steve, here, is going to give me a million dollars (big laugh), yes a million dollars to say that I can't hear his voice when I know I can and so do you. I'd take the money, here, because we all are aware of an additional fact, we all know what I've said is not true. I'd be acting so I can have the money. But if we did not know I was playing a role and that I was paid to say that I could not hear when actually I could, that would be a corruption of my personal truth and a breach of trust and community that could cause trouble....for example, you might say things aloud that you did not want me to know because you were misled to believe that I could not hear your voice. You'd be at risk with respect to what I did with the information I actually heard. Steve would have bought and owned my personal truth as well as misled you for his purposes. How else do you think he got the million dollars, (big laugh).

Me getting paid to lie to you is corrupt. It's also the way many parts of Industrial Society operate. They pay us or otherwise reward us to be unreasonable, we lose our integrity and, feeling bad, we tranquilize ourselves or become excessive to relieve the discomfort or to get into feeling better. As we find this works and is rewarding, we addict to doing it. We also addict to knowingly becoming expensively addicted and/or making money by selling addictive substances. Meanwhile, we have given our power and integrity to those who have hurt and are corrupting us, a destructive vicious circle. Tom Lehrer joked about living this way, "Life is like a sewer, what you get out of it depends upon what you put into it."

ANTIDOTE FOR CORRUPTION

What I will teach you today is how to put Nature as organic higher power into the sewer parts of your mind, to help you compost their contamination and recycle them into purity-making. Nature does this all the time; it's how Nature works. I will give you the ability to use Nature, including your natural senses, as a trustable and rewarding means to gain satisfaction in ways that benefit all, including Nature. It works because the process also helps you determine if what I teach is true and has value for you. You can fully experience, consider and validate it,

VALUE INDEX My degree of attraction to the information on this page:
1   2   3   4   5   6   7   8   9   10
None   Moderate   Strong
IF IMPORTANT, WHY?

ACTIVITY PAGE

RESPONSES write your Validations in the space provided below.

RECORD NOTES, Reactions, Questions, Comments, Drawings, Rubs, Samples

INCREASE AWARENESS Write responses to the activities found in Appendix H

DO POWER ACTIVITIES **Match – Resonate – Appreciate – Trust – Celebrate** *(see Appendix B)*.

OPTION: arrange an onsite workshop with Dr. Cohen 1-360-378-6313

Text References are listed by number in Appendix G with online links.

LEARN MORE Master ECHN: online orientation course www.ecopsych.com/orient.html

PASS IT ON: Increase your expertise by 75%. Teach NHP to another person.

just as we have done here today.

This reminds me of when I was a child and a magician visited our elementary school. He explained in his show that he was going to perform a miracle: 'Miraculously, I am going to make something from nothing,' he said. He first rolled up his sleeves, then opened wide both his hands and twisted them so we could see them, back and front. He asked us if we recognized that that they were bare and empty. We agreed. They were. No doubt about it. The others and I, including our teacher, saw this with our own eyes.

THE MIRACLE

Then came the miracle. Out of nothing, there came something. The magician made a loose fist with one hand and with the other hand he pulled from his fist many scarves of different colors. While he was doing this he repeated, 'You see, I have the power to make the impossible happen."

We all believed his story. Why not? We experienced it, we saw it. *Validate.* The magician said he could perform magic, why should we not believe him? He certainly didn't lie, he did what he said he would and could do. This built and established our trust in him. Sight, Sound and understanding stories, our Literacy, are just a few of the 54 natural senses that our body and spirit inherit in order to register the world around and in us *(Appendix E, 6)*.

If the magician's label or story had been honest, or had his integrity invited us to come closer or touch and feel his hands, we would have known what we needed to know about his 'miracle.' Our senses would have been able to register that he was deceiving us. He would not have corrupted our thinking into trusting him. About sixty years later I became aware of the magician's secret. He had an imitation, hollow plastic thumb placed over his real thumb and he knew we didn't know this. Inside the hollow plastic thumb there was space enough to hide the scarves. So, while his fake-thumb was buried in his fist he pulled his real thumb out from its plastic cover. With his other hand he took the scarves out of the plastic thumb shell while telling us corrupt and deceptive stories about his miraculous powers and empty hands.

Why did the Magician mislead us innocent youngsters? Because he was paid to do it or he liked to do it, it gave him notoriety or pride or power as a professional magician. Somehow it

VALUE INDEX My degree of attraction to the information on this page:

1	2	3	4	5	6	7	8	9	10
	None			Moderate			Strong		

IF IMPORTANT, WHY?

was attractive and rewarding.

Fooling people is how magicians make money and gain prestige. It is entertainment as well as a way the economy works to satisfy our need for entertainment, be we magicians or their audience.

As long as I trusted the magician's label or story I did not get all the facts that I needed. He did nothing to help me as a child think he was a fabricator or help me figure out his use of a fake thumb. He did not encourage me to "impolitely" not trust his word or demonstration, to demand that he let me fully experience his hands through 'transparency,' through my 54 inherent sensory ways of knowing. Somebody said: "Corruption is authority plus monopoly minus transparency."

As a consequence of the Magician withholding information and misleading me, I ended up believing in magic. I don't believe in magic any more, not even Magic Johnson. What I believe is that reasonable, whole life, self-evident experience is the best teacher and that scientific research supports my multi-sensory experiences with nature. This is something that happened in my life. *Validate.* As I describe in my book *Educating, Counseling and Healing With Nature*, I stuck with these facts and have used them to achieve Ph.D's as well as develop books and courses that help folks use the facts effectively (1). *Validate.*

SENSORY GENETICS

There is one more truth we must put on the list before we continue any further." I said. "Do you remember, think, feel or sense that some individual made you study how to sense and feel. Did somebody teach you, or make you read a book about how to do it? Or do you think, instead, that you inherited your sensing and feeling ability in your genetic makeup, that it is part of your natural self in the same way that you nose, eyes or ears are inherently parts of you, parts that give you the ability to register the world directly, in a felt-sense, non-story, pure truth, way?"

Soon the group participants agreed that they were born with their ability to register sensations, that it was genetic to have an immediate, natural, felt-sense way of knowing unadulterated facts about life and their lives, *Validate*".

CHAPTER 2

THE HIDDEN OBVIOUS

ACTIVITY PAGE

RESPONSES write your Validations in the space provided below.

RECORD NOTES, Reactions, Questions, Comments, Drawings, Rubs, Samples

INCREASE AWARENESS Write responses to the activities found in Appendix H

DO POWER ACTIVITIES **Match – Resonate – Appreciate – Trust – Celebrate** *(see Appendix B).*

OPTION: arrange an onsite workshop with Dr. Cohen 1-360-378-6313

Text References are listed by number in Appendix G with online links.

LEARN MORE Master ECHN: online orientation course www.ecopsych.com/orient.html

PASS IT ON: Increase your expertise by 75%. Teach NHP to another person.

CHAPTER 2

THE HIDDEN OBVIOUS

10:24 AM. "Let me share more about myself with you" I said, "I suffered similar corrupting childhood trespasses and injuries to yours, in fact most everybody has in some form since our society is teeming with crazy making and corruption. However, as you can see, I'm not in jail, or homeless, or on welfare, or substance addicted so what I've learned and done will be helpful to you if you use it.

Now, I am going to complete my original opening sentence:

My name is Mike and I have two bodies," I offered. Most of the group looked surprised. I continued, "Planet Earth is my other body. I know this is true because when I think about who or what I would be without my other body, Earth, I feel the pain of loss, anguish and despair. These sensations tell me that 'Earth is my other body' is true for me because its loss registers in my senses and it hurts when I experience its removal from me in my imagination, or in reality. This is not a hallucination. It is a fact for me because, like we just did, I long ago validated that felt-senses that I experienced were my personal truths. The more I think about what it means to not having Earth as my other body, the worse I feel. I also experience this in reality if I separate from my 'other body' by holding my breath for a long period of time. I feel the pain; I'm painfully sure I'm losing contact with the Planet's air. In addition, I know the Planet has the same love of me because if I decide never to breathe again and I pass out, the Planet gives my personal body "natural respiration" and revives me. It treasures my life, your's too. (21). This disconnection discomfort is true for many other separations and sensations such as thirst, hunger, place, community, beauty, reason and gravity. I am aware that this is true for other animals and plants, too (21). For this reason Earth being our other body (Other Body) is included in my PNC Warranty to the world because I experienced it, as have many other people (20). *Validate* including taking a few "get real" slow and deep "Earth-Connecting" breaths and noticing how this Other Body blending feels good while it invigorates and relaxes you . Then be aware of all the other ways in a natural area your Other Body is signaling you. It doesn't need to say a word because it has given you 54 natural senses that sustain you by registering nature's wisdom in a natural area, not in a shopping mall.

VALUE INDEX My degree of attraction to the information on this page:

1	2	3	4	5	6	7	8	9	10
	None			Moderate			Strong		

IF IMPORTANT, WHY?

ACTIVITY PAGE

RESPONSES write your Validations in the space provided below.

RECORD NOTES, Reactions, Questions, Comments, Drawings, Rubs, Samples

INCREASE AWARENESS Write responses to the activities found in Appendix H

DO POWER ACTIVITIES **Match – Resonate – Appreciate – Trust – Celebrate** *(see Appendix B)*.

OPTION: arrange an onsite workshop with Dr. Cohen 1-360-378-6313

Text References are listed by number in Appendix G with online links.

LEARN MORE Master ECHN: online orientation course www.ecopsych.com/orient.html

PASS IT ON: Increase your expertise by 75%. Teach NHP to another person.

Now each of you think about the dance of Earth being your other body. Try it out. What do you think and feel when you imagine being yourself right now minus your other body, Earth including your natural senses like Hunger, Breathing or Sex Awareness being taken away from who you are?" Most of the participants recognized that, like myself, this would leave them hurt, spinning and bewildered. Earth was obviously their other body. Some held their breath until they felt the pain from the air-disconnection they choose to explore.

"Let's take 5 minutes now to walk through the natural area outside slowly while looking around and continually repeating to yourself *'I'm walking through my Other Body.'* What occurs? What benefits do you sense and feel? Is this a reasonable thing to do."

Upon our return, most felt refreshed and it did not take much time or discussion for the participants to acknowledge that I was not crazy, that not only was Earth my other body, it was their other body, also. They, too, could feel the pain of its loss, of missing its refreshment, from just the thought of it being taken away, *Earth being our other body* had to be reasonable. It was as if we were all conscious that every aspect of Earth was dancing its cycles through, in and around us: air, water, food, gravity, temperature, balance, changes, life, people and beauty along with our ability to sense them. We belonged. We felt-sensed from each other and ourselves that biologically we and Earth were really one body, *Validate*, and that this was also part of the PNC Warranty.

One participant upon return shared that he did not experience Earth as his other body, that he was whole onto himself and to everything he did or sensed as an organism was within his own natural genetics and personhood, so his whole body was all he had or needed. I agreed that what he said made sense and then added in exaggeration, "In fact, your body can and has done this so well that you have taught or given the body of a dog or mouse these same living organism abilities that you have, sight, hearing, reacting, hunger. How did you do that, and if you didn't, who or what did?" Slowly a glazed look came over his eyes, they almost crossed and he replied, "Oh, I see what you are getting at." I continued teasing him, "How does you body create the genetic makeup of the Dog, or the rest of life." "I get it," he responded, "Yes,

ACTIVITY PAGE

RESPONSES write your Validations in the space provided below.

RECORD NOTES, Reactions, Questions, Comments, Drawings, Rubs, Samples

INCREASE AWARENESS Write responses to the activities found in Appendix H

DO POWER ACTIVITIES **Match – Resonate – Appreciate – Trust – Celebrate** *(see Appendix B).*

OPTION: arrange an onsite workshop with Dr. Cohen 1-360-378-6313

Text References are listed by number in Appendix G with online links.

LEARN MORE Master ECHN: online orientation course www.ecopsych.com/orient.html

PASS IT ON: Increase your expertise by 75%. Teach NHP to another person.

I can see that Earth is my "Other Body, wow, it makes sense now. I can't wait to see what happens next time I try the activity outside"

ECHN empowers you to act from these classic observations:

"What greater grief than the loss of one's native land." - **Euripides circa 450 B.C.**

"Ishi, (the last hunter-gather Native American) was sure he knew the cause of our discontent. It stemmed from an excessive amount of indoor time. 'It is not a man's nature to be too much indoors." - **Theodora Kroeber circa 1965**

The result of the activity and its discussion was that we confirmed what we discovered by going around the room and having each person state their name and then add that they had another body, that it was Planet Earth and how that felt. "My name is Charley and Earth is my other body. I know this is true for me because I feel reasonable and happy when I experience it." A *Validate* by the group helped us became aware that we all know Earth as our other body followed this. We said, "We all hold in common that Earth is our other body" We knew this was true for us because we had experienced it, unedited, directly through our senses. It made sense to both our bodies. It also made sense because it was not an LSD or other drug induced illusion or dependency with harmful side effects. This common experience unified the group to some extent; they began to help each other increase the health of their individual and collective Other Body while vowing to defend it from injury by the conquering and exploitive ways of Industrial Society.

In summary, I asked them "Isn't the Divine everywhere, can't the nature of your Other Body be your higher power in your 12-step program?"

ECHN empowers you to act from these classic observations:

"Although each particular thing be conditioned by another particular thing to exist in a given way, yet the force whereby each particular thing perseveres in existing follows from the eternal necessity of God's nature." - **Baruch Spinoza circa 1651**

"We belong to the ground. It is our power and we must stay close to it or maybe we will get lost." - **Aborigine (Jennifer Isaacs) circa unknown.**

VALUE INDEX My degree of attraction to the information on this page:

1	2	3	4	5	6	7	8	9	10
None				Moderate			Strong		

IF IMPORTANT, WHY?

ACTIVITY PAGE

RESPONSES write your Validations in the space provided below.

RECORD NOTES, Reactions, Questions, Comments, Drawings, Rubs, Samples

INCREASE AWARENESS Write responses to the activities found in Appendix H

DO POWER ACTIVITIES **Match – Resonate – Appreciate – Trust – Celebrate** *(see Appendix B).*

OPTION: arrange an onsite workshop with Dr. Cohen 1-360-378-6313

Text References are listed by number in Appendix G with online links.

LEARN MORE Master ECHN: online orientation course www.ecopsych.com/orient.html

PASS IT ON: Increase your expertise by 75%. Teach NHP to another person.

WHEN IS NATURE?

10:30 AM "So," I said, "Let me ask you a key question that I'm positive you can answer because you have experienced it as part of your contact with nature. Ready? 'WHEN is, or was, your Other Body?'"

Most said they did not understand the question, others remembered good experiences they had in nature and said they now could see that their Other Body was in and part of those experiences. To them I replied, 'When is or was that happening?' and they gave an approximate date, often in early childhood.

I said, "Think about this: the only answer to the question of 'when' is your other body is 'Now.' You see, what happened in the past no longer exists, it is a memory, a story that you are experiencing in the present, in the immediate moment, and similarly, your Other Body is here, now, too. It and its sensory abilities help your two bodies experience that memory of the past in the singular present. In this way the two are unified as one single point in time. So, in this sense, everything you do or have done only exists in the present. The past and future are simply stories, true or false, about those different times and places, but the stories only exist and are registered by you in the present, in the Now of life. Why is this? Because the dance of all of nature and the universe only exist in the Now, and this includes you and your ability to experience and Validate them since you are part of them. Significantly, in addition, the only time you can influence or change the world or yourself, or Validate, is also in the Now. You, along with your Other Body, your stories and desires, only exist in the Now. In fact, scientists say that Nature is continually creating time and space so we are all part of creation.

What's important to see is that your Other Body is only available to you in the present because that's the only time it exists. If you want its companionship or help, you must include it in what you sense, think, feel and do because, again, all things are simultaneous; we all only exist in the Now. Think about it. The Now is the only time your life dances and that you have access to higher power. So if you want Nature or your Other Body in yourself and others to

VALUE INDEX My degree of attraction to the information on this page:

1	2	3	4	5	6	7	8	9	10
	None				Moderate			Strong	

IF IMPORTANT, WHY?

ACTIVITY PAGE

RESPONSES write your Validations in the space provided below.

RECORD NOTES, Reactions, Questions, Comments, Drawings, Rubs, Samples

INCREASE AWARENESS Write responses to the activities found in Appendix H

DO POWER ACTIVITIES **Match – Resonate – Appreciate – Trust – Celebrate** *(see Appendix B)*.

OPTION: arrange an onsite workshop with Dr. Cohen 1-360-378-6313

Text References are listed by number in Appendix G with online links.

LEARN MORE Master ECHN: online orientation course www.ecopsych.com/orient.html

PASS IT ON: Increase your expertise by 75%. Teach NHP to another person.

help your recovery or your future, you need to make sure your past and present experiences with them are part of the immediate 'higher power' that you turn to.

The greatest thing you can trust in your life is not God, love, honesty or nature. The greatest trustable truth is what you sense and feel in any given moment, in the 'Now' of life, like you right now hear my voice or see each other. *Validate.*

I emphasize the importance of the Now to you because, due to our education and socialization, on average, 99.9 percent of the time we spend thinking and feeling in the Now is disconnected from, and out of tune with, Nature and your Other Body. Our institutions *(Appendix C)* teach us to spend, on average, over 95 percent of our time indoors, separated from our Other Body and it's amazing wisdom that is also ours when we have access to it and use it. That access, too, can only happen in the Now. It's what makes what we sense and feel in the moment true for ourselves. It explains why we can reduce our stress and feel happier from just a short quiet visit to a natural area. Then, without even knowing it, we are making unadulterated sensory Now contact with our Other Body's dance of the eons.

Think of it this way if it helps, the next layer of your body is the over 100 microorganism, web-of-life species that live on your skin. Then the next layer of you is the air, for you live in, not on, our planet as I have warranted *(Appendix A)*.

For my own part, I know I have two bodies because they continually tell me so since a day in 1965 when my years of outdoor experiences reached me fully. They convinced me that there was nothing that I did that Planet Earth did not also do, that if I was a living organism, it was, too, and I was a like a cell in it *(Appendix F)*. We were the singularity of the dance of one living, diverse Being, moment by moment, and I was part of its diversity.

It became obvious to me that the hurt of my childhood in 1936 was discomfort caused by the assault of Earth, my other body, by our unchecked stories of conquest and excessive exploitation of it. I watched as that pain drove and had driven some of my friends and their parents to substance abuse. My family avoided this discomfort to some extent simply because we were "addicted" to getting fulfillment from contact with nature and its values, in and about

VALUE INDEX My degree of attraction to the information on this page:

1	2	3	4	5	6	7	8	9	10
	None				Moderate			Strong	

IF IMPORTANT, WHY?

ACTIVITY PAGE

RESPONSES write your Validations in the space provided below.

RECORD NOTES, Reactions, Questions, Comments, Drawings, Rubs, Samples

INCREASE AWARENESS Write responses to the activities found in Appendix H

DO POWER ACTIVITIES **Match – Resonate – Appreciate – Trust – Celebrate** *(see Appendix B).*

OPTION: arrange an onsite workshop with Dr. Cohen 1-360-378-6313

Text References are listed by number in Appendix G with online links.

LEARN MORE Master ECHN: online orientation course www.ecopsych.com/orient.html

PASS IT ON: Increase your expertise by 75%. Teach NHP to another person.

us and our friends. To my parents, that made sense so they chose to live in an experimental New York City "utopian garden community" developed by Eleanor Roosevelt and Louis Mumford in 1925. Even then, the pain at school injured my relationship with my Mother and the relationship never fully recovered.

Today, the only thing that makes me into two bodies is my thinking and feeling when it entertains a false story that says that the dance that Earth's life dances and the dance that my life dances, are different. They are not. The two dances are part of the total, whole, Dance of Life. They are each a variation of it but identical, they feed it and each other.

The dance of the Other Body of another person is also my dance and we relate with love, care and support when we get to know each other as dancers.

When I ask myself who or what would I be if my other body, Earth, was taken away from me, the answer is that I would be an illusion (2). I would be my attachment to a false story that says our Other Body, Earth, and we are different. I'd be just my name and my thoughts and voice talking to themselves because what makes Earth and me 'two different things' is that I let that incorrect "difference" story influence my thinking and feelings. In other words, I'd be a false story and words alone. I'd be a no-body instead of a two-body that is me, my singular dance of Earth, a beautiful and wise unity (8).

My "logic" for all this is that I sense for sure that time and space are attractive parts of this Universe, which is Nature. This means that if I'm seeking higher power in Nature, as the saying goes: "There's no time (and space) like the present"

ECHN empowers you to act from these classic observations:

> "This earth which is spread out like a map around is but the lining of my inmost soul exposed." **- Henry David Thoreau circa 1850**

> I want to blend with the hills, shrink into them and finally disappear in them. All of nature is in us, all of us is in nature. That is as it should be."
> **- Pete Catches, Sioux medicine man, circa 1985**

VALUE INDEX My degree of attraction to the information on this page:

1	2	3	4	5	6	7	8	9	10
None				Moderate			Strong		

IF IMPORTANT, WHY?

ACTIVITY PAGE

RESPONSES write your Validations in the space provided below.

RECORD NOTES, Reactions, Questions, Comments, Drawings, Rubs, Samples

INCREASE AWARENESS Write responses to the activities found in Appendix H

DO POWER ACTIVITIES **Match – Resonate – Appreciate – Trust – Celebrate** *(see Appendix B)*.

OPTION: arrange an onsite workshop with Dr. Cohen 1-360-378-6313

Text References are listed by number in Appendix G with online links.

LEARN MORE Master ECHN: online orientation course www.ecopsych.com/orient.html

PASS IT ON: Increase your expertise by 75%. Teach NHP to another person.

"Now, let's take 5 minutes to visit our Other Body, the natural area outside, and ride it like the crest of a wave through time and space because that's what it is. We will cancel our out-of-the moment stories by continually repeating 'I'm experiencing my Other Body in this moment." What occurs? What happens if you also repeat 'Unity'. What benefits do you sense or feel?   Keep in mind that you are making them happen because you choose to participate in this higher power, Other Body, connection activity. You are part of it. In addition, you know you can always choose to benefit from this activity again and again. That would make your attraction to do this activity your higher power in action."

Validation Checklist: To help you come into balance, your nature-connecting *Validation* enables you, in to strengthen your awareness of any experience by further inviting nature to help you improve how you think, feel and relate to the world. A Validation includes the fact that Planet Earth is a living organism and that your life dances in and as part of it, like an individual cell of Earth's whole web-of-life dance.

1. Begin your validation through "inspiration" by taking a few deep slow breaths. They bring Earth's atmosphere into you so you sense and feel the connection of your life with your Other Body's web of life. Notice how Earth supports you by bringing your awareness into the moment and calming and energizing you with the joy of nature's wise and powerful dance of the moment (21).

2. Say to yourself, or aloud, about the self-evident truth you have discovered and are validating "I know it is true for me because I experienced it."

3. Seek or notice additional senses, thoughts or feelings that come into play during this validation. Do additional affirmations as time and interest permit: match, resonate, appreciate, trust, celebrate (Appendix B)

4. Thank nature/earth for providing the time and space for this life experience. Share it with others.

ECHN empowers you to act from this classic observation:

"It is quite clear to me after several years in the environmental movement that all physical problems of man's impact on the environment - pollution of the air and waters, the desecration of the land, the contamination of the food chain - all start within the environment of man's mind." - **Maurice Strong circa 1989**

ACTIVITY PAGE

RESPONSES write your Validations in the space provided below.

RECORD NOTES, Reactions, Questions, Comments, Drawings, Rubs, Samples

INCREASE AWARENESS Write responses to the activities found in Appendix H

DO POWER ACTIVITIES **Match – Resonate – Appreciate – Trust – Celebrate** *(see Appendix B).*

OPTION: arrange an onsite workshop with Dr. Cohen 1-360-378-6313

Text References are listed by number in Appendix G with online links.

LEARN MORE Master ECHN: online orientation course www.ecopsych.com/orient.html

PASS IT ON: Increase your expertise by 75%. Teach NHP to another person.

OUR NATURAL SELF: LIVING WITH OUR OTHER BODY

We are biologically born to live in tribal wilderness communities and we are genetically compatible with their citizens today. In general, within these nature-based cultures the average primitive is competent and organic in nearly every activity his tribe and family engage in. He or she is an expert hunter or gatherer, a keen observer of nature, a craftsman who can make a kit bag of tools and weapons, a herder who knows the habits and needs of cattle and a direct participant in a variety of tribal rituals and ceremonies. He is likely to be well versed in the legends, tales, and proverbs of his people, more so than most of us. He participates more fully and directly in the whole of life as an actively participating, complete person, not mediated, not vicariously or as a consumer. Most of his natural senses are engaged and satisfied by producing the happiness of survival in balance. In contrast, few of us are competent in organics, much less expert at more than a few activities that contribute to the functioning of our mass artificial society. We are dependent and skilled in media stories, not real life organic relationships. To make things worse, as technologies become more complex and society increasingly fragmented, we become less self-sufficient with reduced self-worth or esteem. We have lost our ancestral knowledge and confidence of how to survive in balance in the Earth so a prejudice against and fear of nature as death lies at the base of our "civilized" psyches. We learn to ignore nature as our caring mother Earth, our greatest life-support, Other Body friend. Our transition from nomadic foraging in new habitats to agricultural and technological civilizations that artificially imitate the life-supportive tropics constitute the original displacement, dispossession and alienation of people from their unifying survival base accompanied by the inequality of women. We have lost leisure time, natural birth control, intimate decision-making, appropriate material goods, a sense of global community and joining together for food gathering and ceremonies rather than warring against other groups that often included relatives. The sensory disassociation and frustration from these hurtful losses underlies our disorders. This explains the urgent need for nature reconnecting activities. We presently pay ourselves to addictively build and live in a socially and environmentally destructive shoe that does not fit us. The more we do this, the more painful the shoe becomes. We have a great need to simultaneously learn to think like nature works, overcome our addictions and make organic shoes.

ACTIVITY PAGE

RESPONSES write your Validations in the space provided below.

RECORD NOTES, Reactions, Questions, Comments, Drawings, Rubs, Samples

INCREASE AWARENESS Write responses to the activities found in Appendix H

DO POWER ACTIVITIES **Match – Resonate – Appreciate – Trust – Celebrate** *(see Appendix B).*

OPTION: arrange an onsite workshop with Dr. Cohen 1-360-378-6313 Text References are listed by number in Appendix G with online links.

LEARN MORE Master ECHN: online orientation course www.ecopsych.com/orient.html

PASS IT ON: Increase your expertise by 75%. Teach NHP to another person.

AN ADDITIONAL OTHER BODY ACTIVITY *(time and interest permitting)*

The words 'psyche' and 'spirit' are ancient names for air. Green plants produce oxygen, the part of air that we breathe, the part that sustains our lives. Air is a product and part of our Other Body, Earth and so is our sensory desire to breathe. We call the breathing process and feeling Respiration, meaning re-spiriting (21).

Approach an attractive green plant in this area and have your sense of Consciousness tell yourself to stop breathing. Then actually stop breathing as its verbal command has requested. This disconnects an important part of your personal body from your Other Body. Notice the disruptive natural feeling of suffocation (#25 pain) that shortly comes into play and intelligently asks you to reconnect by breathing again.

Only allow yourself breathe again by holding onto or embracing part of the plant because it produces the oxygen you need for survival. This lets your Other Body natural senses feelingly bring to your story-brain consciousness and sense of appreciation that the plant supports you. Note the rewarding feeling from your natural sense of Respiration.

Release the plant, stop breathing and see what happens as you walk further. Continue repeating this activity with additional plant connections to continue learning from it.

Remember that our relationship with our Other Body is balanced and fair, for example, as we breathe the oxygen it makes, it breathes the carbon di-oxide that we make.

There are 160 Other Body connection activities that help us habitually re-connect 160 disconnections from nature, in and around others and us and help us think like the perfections of our Other Body work. Each resembles playing "Hide and Seek" and validating what is discovered about our self being our Other Body. All one needs to do is be attracted to learn, use and teach these activities and *Validate* their truths as they find them. You find many additional truths as you teach the activities to others. The key is to simply choose to follow your attraction to do the activities and then do them.

Visit the many links at our Survey of Participants (5) to view the results of ECHN activities for individuals who were/are following their attractions to do it and did it. Visit www.ecopsych. com/orient.html if you want to master how to do it.

VALUE INDEX My degree of attraction to the information on this page:

1	2	3	4	5	6	7	8	9	10
	None				Moderate			Strong	

IF IMPORTANT, WHY?

58

CHAPTER 3

THE SECRET SOURCE
OF TWO-NESS

ACTIVITY PAGE

RESPONSES write your Validations in the space provided below.

RECORD NOTES, Reactions, Questions, Comments, Drawings, Rubs, Samples

INCREASE AWARENESS Write responses to the activities found in Appendix H

DO POWER ACTIVITIES **Match – Resonate – Appreciate – Trust – Celebrate** *(see Appendix B)*.

OPTION: arrange an onsite workshop with Dr. Cohen 1-360-378-6313

Text References are listed by number in Appendix G with online links.

LEARN MORE Master ECHN: online orientation course www.ecopsych.com/orient.html

PASS IT ON: Increase your expertise by 75%. Teach NHP to another person.

CHAPTER 3
THE SECRET SOURCE OF TWO-NESS

10:35 AM "For the next 10 minutes," I said, "Let's explore another fact that I warrant to be true about our other body, Earth (Other Body) and Nature. It is this: until we discover otherwise, with the exception of humanity and the like, neither our Other Body nor any other part of Nature is literate. In other words, the dance of the natural world, in and around us, does not have the ability to read, write, map or articulate how it works or what to do. It just self-organizes its dance in balance and dances it continually, one moment at a time. It can commune things via relationship energies, *but not fluidly speak or write them as stories* (2).

Things in our Other Body innately know and gain vital information from each other by their sensitivities to each other's presence in the dance on sub-atomic to galactic levels, not by the literacy of hearing or reading descriptions of the dance. The latter are abstracts. Abstracts are literary short cuts; they are not the real thing.

ECHN empowers you to act from this classic observation:

"The name that can be named is not the eternal name. The Nameless is the origin of Heaven and Earth."
- **Lao Tzu circa 600 B.C.**

Our Old Brain, or Mammalian Brain, registers senses and feelings. Sensations are not fiction. They are real. Our New Brain sense of Literacy registers our Old Brain sensitivities and translates them into factual stories. It imaginatively creates new fictional stories, as well. In either case, stories are abstracts of what they describe. In this way *they are usually removed, even when they convey facts* about our Other Body. (10)

"I once asked two elementary school girls if they could answer a simple math question that I had seen on a critical thinking math aptitude/intelligence test. This logical reasoning question

VALUE INDEX My degree of attraction to the information on this page:

1	2	3	4	5	6	7	8	9	10
	None			Moderate			Strong		

IF IMPORTANT, WHY?

ACTIVITY PAGE

RESPONSES write your Validations in the space provided below.

RECORD NOTES, Reactions, Questions, Comments, Drawings, Rubs, Samples

INCREASE AWARENESS Write responses to the activities found in Appendix H

DO POWER ACTIVITIES **Match – Resonate – Appreciate – Trust – Celebrate** *(see Appendix B)*.

OPTION: arrange an onsite workshop with Dr. Cohen 1-360-378-6313

Text References are listed by number in Appendix G with online links.

LEARN MORE Master ECHN: online orientation course www.ecopsych.com/orient.html

PASS IT ON: Increase your expertise by 75%. Teach NHP to another person.

is used to help determine our mathematical ability or our competency to qualify for the rewards of better job, higher salary or greater prestige and self-worth. Here's the question:

'If you count a dog's tail as one of its legs, how many legs does a normal dog have?'

With smiles, both girls proudly responded "five" and looked at me as if I had asked a dumb question.

'Yes,' I replied, "And have you ever seen a real dog? How many legs does it have?"

"Four'

"Is its tail one of its legs?'

'No, silly,'

"Well then, isn't your mathematics answer misleading or incorrect, doesn't a real dog only have four legs?' "

As they thought about my question, sadness filled the girl's faces. They thought they answered the question wrong or that I said they were wrong, or their teacher was bad. The younger girl was about to cry.

Our stringently learned 'five-leg dog story,' New Brain's extreme *disconnection* from thinking with our usually neglected yet inherent Old-Brain, Other Body, "4-leg dog" sensory way of knowing, causes serious deficiencies in the way we relate to ourselves, each other and the global ecosystem (10). As the girls demonstrated, this occurs at a very early age.

Most of us have been conditioned to believe that 2 + 2 = 4 is more true or factual than our sensation of Thirst or Smell.

ACTIVITY PAGE

RESPONSES write your Validations in the space provided below.

RECORD NOTES, Reactions, Questions, Comments, Drawings, Rubs, Samples

INCREASE AWARENESS Write responses to the activities found in Appendix H

DO POWER ACTIVITIES **Match – Resonate – Appreciate – Trust – Celebrate** *(see Appendix B).*

OPTION: arrange an onsite workshop with Dr. Cohen 1-360-378-6313

Text References are listed by number in Appendix G with online links.

LEARN MORE Master ECHN: online orientation course www.ecopsych.com/orient.html

PASS IT ON: Increase your expertise by 75%. Teach NHP to another person.

NINE LEG THINKING

It makes sense to take the time to gather sensory, 4-leg information from the real dog, (our Other Body,) and reasonably translate and blend it with our nature-disconnected 5-leg story world to produce 9-leg, whole life thinking. That makes how we think and feel more organic. It enables us to fully benefit from the contribution of story and sensations to produce more balanced, realistic and whole thoughts, feelings and relationships.

ECHN empowers you to act from these classic observations:

> "Aristotle thought there were eight legs on a fly and wrote it down. For centuries scholars were content to quote his authority. Apparently, not one of them was curious enough to impale a fly and count its six legs." - **Stuart Chase circa 1942**

> "An actually existing fly is more important than a possibly existing angel."
> - **Ralph Waldo Emerson circa 1862**

"Because the web-of-life and its members are non-literate, the PNC warranty guarantees that Nature does not have the ability to create misleading stories or produce the destructive effects of stories that erode, rather than support the life of Earth, our Other Body. Think about it. Can any of you give an example or share an experience that shows Earth is literate?"

Nobody in the group could do this and in order for them to further trust what they already knew, I had them go out in the nearby natural area for five minutes and explore to see if anything there was actually literate. We found that nothing that was linguistic, nothing that could articulate, read or write so, upon return, we added "non-literate" as a trustable fact about or Other Body to our growing list of facts. *Validate.*

ECHN empowers you to act from these classic observations:
> "At night, I open the window and ask the moon to come and press its face against mine, breathe into me. Close the language door and open the love window. The moon won't use the door, only the window." - **Jedaluddin Rumi, circa 1257**

> "I am the Lorax. I speak for the trees. I speak for the trees for the trees have no tongues." - **Dr. Seuss 1971**

VALUE INDEX My degree of attraction to the information on this page:

1	2	3	4	5	6	7	8	9	10
	None			Moderate			Strong		

IF IMPORTANT, WHY?

ACTIVITY PAGE

RESPONSES write your Validations in the space provided below.

RECORD NOTES, Reactions, Questions, Comments, Drawings, Rubs, Samples

INCREASE AWARENESS Write responses to the activities found in Appendix H

DO POWER ACTIVITIES **Match – Resonate – Appreciate – Trust – Celebrate** *(see Appendix B).*

OPTION: arrange an onsite workshop with Dr. Cohen 1-360-378-6313

Text References are listed by number in Appendix G with online links.

LEARN MORE Master ECHN: online orientation course www.ecopsych.com/orient.html

PASS IT ON: Increase your expertise by 75%. Teach NHP to another person.

NINE LEG LABELING

NOTE: The challenge in this book is to recognize that the literacy of and in its text is foreign to what it is trying to convey about and to our non-literate Other Body. For this reason, the text tries to help you do the activities in natural areas so our Other Body can teach us what we need to know via its sensory lnaguage that we have inheherited and have been taught to ignore. This process is somewhat like teaching a blind person to recognize the color green.

Next I said, "A dance is not a noun, it's an action, a verb that has spirit. Its literate name or label is more accurate when it becomes an action/verb. You can do this by adding 'ing' to it and calling the dance 'dancing.' And our words can convey its spirit by adding "ness" to it so it becomes our whole essence or spirit, our 'wholeness' or 'danceness.' This helps our sense of Consciousness acknowledge our Other Body everywhere for what it is, for example a tree becomes "my tree body" "treeness" or "treeing," a frog becomes "my frog body" "frogness" or "frogging," and each or us becomes the unifying essence of our 'bodyness' 'oneness' or 'being'. "

"Now let's go back to the natural area and experiment with adding 'body' 'ness' and 'ing' to the name of each thing you see and *Validate.*" Upon their return, many participants noted that this was helpful. It added energy to their Other Body so it became more expressive and they became more aware of their loving kinship with its 'being' and 'aliveness.' "

Some of the participants expressed appreciation for making their Other Body so quickly accessible to their awareness."

THE SELF-IDENTITY ACTIVITY: WHERE DOES NATURE END AND YOURSELF BEGIN? (9)

1) This NAE activity gave each individual in an ECHN study group a few moments to recognize that they are part of nature and then obtain consent from an attractive natural area to visit it. Then, they did the activity alone,

2) The spent two minutes finding natural attractions in that area.

VALUE INDEX My degree of attraction to the information on this page:

1	2	3	4	5	6	7	8	9	10
	None			Moderate			Strong		

IF IMPORTANT, WHY?

ACTIVITY PAGE

RESPONSES write your Validations in the space provided below.

RECORD NOTES, Reactions, Questions, Comments, Drawings, Rubs, Samples

INCREASE AWARENESS Write responses to the activities found in Appendix H

DO POWER ACTIVITIES **Match – Resonate – Appreciate – Trust – Celebrate** *(see Appendix B).*

OPTION: arrange an onsite workshop with Dr. Cohen 1-360-378-6313

Text References are listed by number in Appendix G with online links.

LEARN MORE Master ECHN: online orientation course www.ecopsych.com/orient.html

PASS IT ON: Increase your expertise by 75%. Teach NHP to another person.

3) They thank each attraction for being there and consenting to make its attractive presence available for this activity. (See Chapter 5)

4) The individual then attempts to discover more about who they personally are as an individual by asking the whole of nature's dance in the natural area "*At what point do you stop and do I start, how are we different or separate?*"

5) Upon sharing the responses that appeared in this setting, the group concluded that the point of separate individuality is that *a person can think, build and relate with words and the natural area cannot do this.*

Can you guarantee, as does the author of this page and ECHN, that:

"Planet Earth is my other body. I base this upon what I sense and feel when my literate self asks: 'Who or what would I think, feel or be if something severed or tore my Earth body away from me, that it was gone, that I could not experience it?' I feel real sadness, loss, anguish and horror and they are sensory truths for me, I experience and validate them. How could this be if Earth was not my other body? Why otherwise would I experience a calling to breathe air after I started to hold my breath, or thirsty when I separate from water? Why do I feel and think better when I spend time in natural areas or when I call trees my 'tree body' rather than my 'resource,' 'slave' or 'enemy.' These 'organic truths' urge me to help others use ECHN to discover and enjoy Planet Earth as their other body and increase their and its well-being. Just like a dog has four legs, not five, for folks who trust the truth of their experiences, (such as a tail is not a leg) sensory connections with Earth can provide or are nature-connected higher power. Each experience is like going on an organic renewing vacation that provides the happiness of reasonable rewards."

Are you willing to modify and/or share the critical statement, above, with the world? What would you say?

ACTIVITY PAGE

RESPONSES write your Validations in the space provided below.

RECORD NOTES, Reactions, Questions, Comments, Drawings, Rubs, Samples

INCREASE AWARENESS Write responses to the activities found in Appendix H

DO POWER ACTIVITIES **Match – Resonate – Appreciate – Trust – Celebrate** *(see Appendix B).*

OPTION: arrange an onsite workshop with Dr. Cohen 1-360-378-6313

Text References are listed by number in Appendix G with online links.

LEARN MORE Master ECHN: online orientation course www.ecopsych.com/orient.html

PASS IT ON: Increase your expertise by 75%. Teach NHP to another person.

SELF-DISCOVERY ACTIVITY:

If I am part of nature's dance and Nature does not use words, how does my nature know itself and its individuality as a wordless natural dancer, or as me?
(Optional, time and interest permitting)

This NAE activity helps an individual further explore self-evidence.

Our sense of touch *Appendix E* (6) is a natural attraction to have the world register in us and help us recognize it and relate to it in a mutually beneficial way that strengthens nature's dance, in and around us. (Touch consists of as many as 22 different inherent senses and sensitivities blending such as temperature, form, size, motion, texture, etc.)

1. Using your best thinking and attention, have one finger touch a material object and become aware of what natural attraction sensation is consciously registering in you by doing this. For example, touch a desk or a tree and be aware of what you feel with eyes open and then closed. (SUGGESTION: Also touch a loose part of the clothing you are wearing so that your body beneath it does not feel you touching it).

2. Repeat doing this but this time touch some natural part of your body. Become aware of what new natural attraction sensations are consciously registering in you by doing this. For example, touch your ankle and be aware of what your finger and your ankle feel with eyes open and then closed. (SUGGESTION: Also touch and Validate the same, as in #1 above, (Touch part of the clothing you are wearing hard enough so that your body beneath it does feel you touching it).

3. Can you recognize that a major difference exists between 1 and 2 above? You might want to repeat them several times.

    In 1 you felt something in one way, via your finger.
    In 2 you felt sensed two things, what your finger sensed and also what the part of you that you touched sensed when you touched it. For example, your finger could feel your ankle

ACTIVITY PAGE

RESPONSES write your Validations in the space provided below.

RECORD NOTES, Reactions, Questions, Comments, Drawings, Rubs, Samples

INCREASE AWARENESS Write responses to the activities found in Appendix H

DO POWER ACTIVITIES **Match – Resonate – Appreciate – Trust – Celebrate** *(see Appendix B).*

OPTION: arrange an onsite workshop with Dr. Cohen 1-360-378-6313

Text References are listed by number in Appendix G with online links.

LEARN MORE Master ECHN: online orientation course www.ecopsych.com/orient.html

PASS IT ON: Increase your expertise by 75%. Teach NHP to another person.

while your ankle could feel your finger. *Validate.*

4. Can you recognize that even if you could not talk or think in verbal language, you would still be able to register 1 and 2 in some distinct way? That the natural attraction sensations themselves communicated sensible knowledge? That this eliminates the possibility of adulterated information creating misinformation because there is no story involved that could be misleading?

5. Can you recognize that your ability to apply the concept of "1" and "2" to your experience further helps you register it? Numerical or verbal abstracting adds to our ability to register the environment. It does not, however, accurately replace it. In people, math and words can be part of, but not all of the whole.

6. Can you conclude from this sensory self-evidence activity that self-evidence produces worthwhile knowledge? That one way to distinguish yourself from your surroundings is that when you touch yourself, as 2 above, you sense two things and when you touch your surroundings, as 1 above, you sense one thing.

If you breathe directly on your finger under your nose, you can immediately discover your individuality. Your attraction to do this connects with what your finger feels, your nose feels, as well as your natural attraction to breathe for survival (Sense #21)

7. Can you distinguish that there is a sensory difference between experience 1 and 2? Does this bring to mind the value or significance of sensory, non-verbal, self-evidence? If so, you have improved how you will know the remaining moments of your life.

ECHN empowers you to act from this classic observation:

> "Nothing in all Nature is more certain than the fact that no single thing or event can stand alone. It is attached to all that has gone before it, and it will remain attached to all that will follow it. It was born of some cause, and so it must be followed by some effect in an endless chain." - **Julian P. Johnson**

VALUE INDEX My degree of attraction to the information on this page:

1	2	3	4	5	6	7	8	9	10
None				Moderate				Strong	

IF IMPORTANT, WHY?

CHAPTER 4

EXPLORING THE NATURAL
ATTRACTION DANCE

CHAPTER 4
EXPLORING THE NATURAL ATTRACTION DANCE

10:50 AM. I said to the group "There is a presently existing 'Attraction Fact' that we should assure ourselves is a trustable truth for us. It is not just a corrupt 'story' truth like the falsehood that tells us we live on Planet Earth instead of whole-life informing us that Earth is our Other Body and that we live in it and are part of its totality.

The established "Attraction Fact" states that attraction is something that draws one object towards another and can attach attracted things. *Validate.* This is important to know because the truth of the PNC model we are learning today includes a guarantee that until somebody proves otherwise, in our scientific-based 'Standard Universe' all things are, and are held together by, attraction, from sub-atomics to galaxies to the Universe itself since its beginning of time and space in the Big Bang.

In my ECHN model, the Big Bang is/was a *self-contained* seed of immense attraction energy whose origins are unknown and theoretical, God or otherwise, for they are stories. We were not there to experience them at the time so we can't validate the seed's 'maker.' However, its origins don't matter for we know the seed worked. We know this because we can sense it. *The Universe including us, are it right now.* Your attraction to hear more about this or to the next thing I might say is also it. We are all part of and expressions of our attraction-based Universe.

As the Big Bang seed expanded, it cooled as it was attracted to grow into more and more attractive diversity (11). The dance of the seed's attraction energy formed and continues to form the time, space and content of our Universe.

If it helps, think of Natural Attraction as the scientific essence of love, beauty, enlightenment, nirvana or dharma in the Standard Universe. If you appreciate the scientific thinking, skill and passion that went into making your computer, car, phone, TV, or blender, you'll love using that same natural genius in you to better your life by bettering the whole of life. Until

VALUE INDEX My degree of attraction to the information on this page:
1   2   3   4   5   6   7   8   9   10
None   Moderate   Strong
IF IMPORTANT, WHY?

ACTIVITY PAGE

RESPONSES write your Validations in the space provided below.

RECORD NOTES, Reactions, Questions, Comments, Drawings, Rubs, Samples

INCREASE AWARENESS Write responses to the activities found in Appendix H

DO POWER ACTIVITIES **Match – Resonate – Appreciate – Trust – Celebrate** *(see Appendix B).*

OPTION: arrange an onsite workshop with Dr. Cohen 1-360-378-6313

Text References are listed by number in Appendix G with online links.

LEARN MORE Master ECHN: online orientation course www.ecopsych.com/orient.html

PASS IT ON: Increase your expertise by 75%. Teach NHP to another person.

further evidence is found to the contrary, this natural attraction observation is as true as the Sun being the center of our solar system."

ECHN empowers you to act from this classic observation:

"I thank God's will to begin this world with the independent Big Bang attraction seed of NNIAAL (12) and the desire of its dance to create and enjoy attractive relationships through the eons (11)." - **Project NatureConnect Student**

From 78 years of experience and study I guarantee in writing that, as part of our Universe, Natural Attraction includes the original energy of the Higgs Boson Big Bang 'seed' (13). In the beginning, it was attracted to cool, self-organize and grow into the dance of the "unifying binding field" long predicted in physics by Albert Einstein.

During any immediate moment, the original attraction energy is the natural attraction essence that is found attractively dancing throughout the 'Standard Universe.' This includes the thoughts, senses, feelings, intelligence and relationships of our body, mind and spirit as part of the Universe. Until you genuinely experience otherwise, it is the safest of bets to build on this truth if you want attractive results (4).

Natural Attraction is the fundamental of all sensations, attractions, ideas and memories of the past, present or future along with our attractive ability to relate to and with them. As John Muir said 'When we try to pick out anything by itself, we find it hitched to everything else in the Universe.' Natural Attraction is the hitching agent.

Since 1974, many have tried but nobody has yet proven me wrong about Natural Attraction being fundamental and in 2012 the discovery of the Higgs Boson Big Bang attraction particle by CERN physicists confirmed it and in 2014 the Big Bang explosion of the Gravity wave (11). For this reason, my Warranty attests and guarantees that Natural Attraction is the dancing

VALUE INDEX My degree of attraction to the information on this page:

1	2	3	4	5	6	7	8	9	10
None				Moderate				Strong	

IF IMPORTANT, WHY?

ACTIVITY PAGE

RESPONSES write your Validations in the space provided below.

RECORD NOTES, Reactions, Questions, Comments, Drawings, Rubs, Samples

INCREASE AWARENESS Write responses to the activities found in Appendix H

DO POWER ACTIVITIES **Match – Resonate – Appreciate – Trust – Celebrate** *(see Appendix B).*

OPTION: arrange an onsite workshop with Dr. Cohen 1-360-378-6313

Text References are listed by number in Appendix G with online links.

LEARN MORE Master ECHN: online orientation course www.ecopsych.com/orient.html

PASS IT ON: Increase your expertise by 75%. Teach NHP to another person.

essence of the universe and is found everywhere."

'We are not throwing $10 billion down this tube for nothing. We're exploring the very forefront of physics and cosmology with the CERN Large Hadron Collider because we want to have a window on creation; we want to recreate a tiny piece of Genesis to unlock some of the greatest secrets of the universe.' - **Michio Kaku circa 2010**

Our selves, including our Other Body, along with everything else, are diverse variations of the Natural Attraction Dance of Nature attractively dancing its way through time and space (9).

Participants' reactions to this included:

 "If God's will made the Natural Attraction Seed to cool and grow into becoming our attractive Universe and Planet, then for me to ignore Natural Attraction goes against God's will. That's a sin."

"This affirms my attraction to let genuine connection with nature, not God, be a source of Higher Power for me in my 12-Step Program. My senses tell me it is real, it feels right and makes sense. It helps me ignore those folks in the program that hassle me about this."

Our selves including our Other Body, along with everything else, are diverse variations of the Natural Attraction Dance of Nature attractively dancing its way through time and space (9).

ECHN empowers you to act from these classic observations:

"Always think of the universe as one living organism, with a single substance, and a single soul." - **Marcus Aurelius circa 161 A.D.**

"If you want to make an apple pie from scratch, you must first create the universe."
- **Carl Sagan circa 2009**

Everything and everybody is a Natural Attraction Dancer except for the stories that say that this truth is not true. Believing or being trained, indoctrinated or addicted to these false stories is the heart of our troubles. So let's go outside, to our Other Body, and sense, see and

VALUE INDEX My degree of attraction to the information on this page:
1   2   3   4   5   6   7   8   9   10
    None   Moderate   Strong
IF IMPORTANT, WHY?

ACTIVITY PAGE

RESPONSES write your Validations in the space provided below.

RECORD NOTES, Reactions, Questions, Comments, Drawings, Rubs, Samples

INCREASE AWARENESS Write responses to the activities found in Appendix H

DO POWER ACTIVITIES **Match – Resonate – Appreciate – Trust – Celebrate** *(see Appendix B).*

OPTION: arrange an onsite workshop with Dr. Cohen 1-360-378-6313

Text References are listed by number in Appendix G with online links.

LEARN MORE Master ECHN: online orientation course www.ecopsych.com/orient.html

PASS IT ON: Increase your expertise by 75%. Teach NHP to another person.

feel what it has to say.

Take five minutes to visit this natural area and try to find or remember there anything whose essence is or was not natural attraction in its atoms and energy, yesterday, today and forever until proven otherwise."

When the group returned to the classroom, no surprise, nobody had found anything whose essence was not natural attraction. *Validate.* However a few had found some important questions.

One question was that although a participant knew that fire was the dance of natural attraction in action, he was not attracted to getting burned by a fire nearby for when he got too close to it, it got too hot. I explained that some of our 54 natural senses, like pain, mental distress and fear are attractions that help our Other Body, Earth, recognize that we should seek other attractions instead of increasing our risk or injury where we are in danger *Appendix E #25-27*. This is an attractive survival quality. It is attractive to have such attraction guidance in conjunction with the sense of Temperature for without it, as in this case, one might get seriously burned.

Another question was why a building made of the atomic attractions in steel and cement sometimes felt invasive or foreign and discomforting. I replied that the "human-built environment" is our Other Body that has been managed, conquered, exploited and molded by our nature-disconnected story world into a non-organic, human-made, artificial product. Our Other Body and Nature's Dance is defenseless against such stories when they become excessive because the Dance is non-literate, stories don't register. However, our 54 sensitivities, what we sense and feel about a story, do register.

We are trained to be eco-zombies. Desensitized, we ignore our Other Body's non-literate, sensory callings that would otherwise balance and purify our ways, as exemplified by the ways of organic farming. In our central way of thinking, it is as if us connecting with nature is like having an illicit affair.

The built environment becomes runaway because our story world dismisses Earth's sensory

VALUE INDEX My degree of attraction to the information on this page:

1	2	3	4	5	6	7	8	9	10
	None			Moderate			Strong		

IF IMPORTANT, WHY?

ACTIVITY PAGE

RESPONSES write your Validations in the space provided below.

RECORD NOTES, Reactions, Questions, Comments, Drawings, Rubs, Samples

INCREASE AWARENESS Write responses to the activities found in Appendix H

DO POWER ACTIVITIES **Match – Resonate – Appreciate – Trust – Celebrate** *(see Appendix B)*.

OPTION: arrange an onsite workshop with Dr. Cohen 1-360-378-6313

Text References are listed by number in Appendix G with online links.

LEARN MORE Master ECHN: online orientation course www.ecopsych.com/orient.html

PASS IT ON: Increase your expertise by 75%. Teach NHP to another person.

signals that would ordinarily help the thinking and feeling of a human to know themselves as a dancer in equilibrium with the whole of nature's dance in and around themselves and the dance of other's. This is also true for all unadulterated Dancers, including beavers and ants; they are also dedicated builders."

Some participant responses to this were

> "We are skilled criminals, we can hide from Society that we are doing activities that re-connect us with our Other Body"

> "As organized street gang members we can protect our Other Body from further harm"

NNIAAL: BODY MIND AND SPRIT

A significant aspect of the essence of Nature's Attraction Dance that I mentioned to the participants is found in the acronym NNIAAL (12). I told them that it's not a name or label, that it's a reminder. I use NNIAAL to bring to mind that we know now, from genuine contact experience, that the Big Bang seed contained the elements of our Other Body, elements whose manifestation we can find and beneficially enjoy as parts of our Other Body today. They are: **Nameless** (non-literate), **Now, Intelligent, Attractive, Aliveness, Love**. (NNIAAL). I gave them, and give you, a link to look further into this form of higher power http://www.ecopsych.com/earthstories101.html.

NNIAAL is a total form of love that, in humanity, gives us the choice of separating platonic love from romantic love. For this reason seeking NNIAAL in nature is helpful in sustaining marriage or partnering.

If some or all of the elements of NNIAAL feel accurate to you, be sure to *Validate* them to get all that they give to your Other Body.

Too often, we overlook that the natural attraction energy dance of the universe is the essence of nature's remarkable powers on our planet. Those powers are true to life energy; they are not imaginary higher power.

VALUE INDEX My degree of attraction to the information on this page:

1	2	3	4	5	6	7	8	9	10
None				Moderate			Strong		

IF IMPORTANT, WHY?

ACTIVITY PAGE

RESPONSES write your Validations in the space provided below.

RECORD NOTES, Reactions, Questions, Comments, Drawings, Rubs, Samples

INCREASE AWARENESS Write responses to the activities found in Appendix H

DO POWER ACTIVITIES **Match – Resonate – Appreciate – Trust – Celebrate** *(see Appendix B)*.

OPTION: arrange an onsite workshop with Dr. Cohen 1-360-378-6313

Text References are listed by number in Appendix G with online links.

LEARN MORE Master ECHN: online orientation course www.ecopsych.com/orient.html

PASS IT ON: Increase your expertise by 75%. Teach NHP to another person.

ECHN empowers you to act from this classic observation:

> "From atoms and molecules to human beings with developed consciousness, all entities feel attraction for one another. . . . attraction is the law of nature."
> - **P.R. Sarkar circa 1970**

> "Life is neither unbiased or indefinable. It is the natural attraction to live. The purpose of life is to support life. – **Michael J. Cohen circa 1985**

Natural Attraction on Earth knows how to grow pure natural areas. They are organic forms of pre-human love that is, has, and gives our Other Body, Earth, the ability to not produce garbage, pollution or excessiveness while, at the same time Earth creates and sustains its balanced optimums of:

> life, diversity, cooperation, equilibrium, purity, composting, beauty, community, wellness, sensitivity, renewal, fairness, organics, spirit, sustainability, self-organization, cycles, self-correction, intelligence, restoration, unification, recycling and love.

Because the above are all phases of Natural Attraction in action, they are all forms and varieties of love that make up our Other Body. When we acknowledge our Other Body we can call on these loves to help us at any time for they are the NNIAAL Big Bang seed in action as higher power today. To accomplish this we learn how to involve ourselves in ECHN activities. They help us create moments that let sensory contact with the dance of our Other Body, around and in us, teach us what we need to know to blend and bind with our Other Body's Dance. Although this simple 'nature literacy' and its balancing powers have long been known, Industrial Society teaches us to ignore it.

Nature can be felt-sensed as the perfection of its attractive way of life rewarding itself for its intelligent way of life surving. Nature's reward is its ability to produce and live in the next moment of its attractive way of life. If nature produced destructive or unreasonable out-comes instead of its perfection, it could be described as being addicted to its way of life.

ECHN empowers you to act from these classic observations:

> "The purpose of life is to live in agreement with nature." - **Zeno, circa 520 BC**

VALUE INDEX My degree of attraction to the information on this page:

1	2	3	4	5	6	7	8	9	10
	None				Moderate			Strong	

IF IMPORTANT, WHY?

ACTIVITY PAGE

RESPONSES write your Validations in the space provided below.

RECORD NOTES, Reactions, Questions, Comments, Drawings, Rubs, Samples

INCREASE AWARENESS Write responses to the activities found in Appendix H

DO POWER ACTIVITIES **Match – Resonate – Appreciate – Trust – Celebrate** *(see Appendix B).*

OPTION: arrange an onsite workshop with Dr. Cohen 1-360-378-6313

Text References are listed by number in Appendix G with online links.

LEARN MORE Master ECHN: online orientation course www.ecopsych.com/orient.html

PASS IT ON: Increase your expertise by 75%. Teach NHP to another person.

"Wind over the lake: the image of inner truth." - **I Ching circa 1200 B.C.**

"In wildness is a civilization other than our own -**Henry David Thoreau circa 1859**

A Summary Key to Reality

As sure as the sun will set, whenever I am aware of my Other Body's dance in the form of a raindrop, a weed or a galaxy, I know them and me to be identical with one exception. It is that I have the additional ability to register and relate to them and their natural attraction dance moment as a story. They don't have that ability. They simply are the dance and that moment, as am I, too, but as a literate being.

An Affirming Natural Attraction Activity

Go to an attractive natural area and ask for its consent to become involved with helping you with this activity. Thank it if it does and go to a few objects or aspects of nature one at a time. For one minute, take hold of each object and pull on it with all your might but do not remove it from the attraction relationships it presently enjoys, or injure its attractive wellness and integrity. Be sure to leave it as you found it. Note what thoughts and feelings come to mind during the minute you are in high energy balanced relationship with each of these objects.

If you hold or pull on water, note that you can't remove your hand from it without it changing by its attraction to you making you wet. This is similar to air changing by being attracted to fill in to where you may have moved your hand.

ECHN empowers you to act from these classic observations:

> "I felt the single blackberry pulling back yet it was also signaling exactly how forceful I should be for both of us to survive. I felt like it was in charge and I respected that. After all, it's intelligent enough to protect itself with thorns while its stems supportively raise each other towards the sun, so smart that it simultaneously turns black, becomes most sweet and makes itself loose enough to pick so that its seeds can be distributed. The dandelion signaled that it wanted to stay where it was. I felt the blade of grass was drawing me into the earth." - **Nature as Higher Power Participant**

VALUE INDEX My degree of attraction to the information on this page:
1   2   3   4   5   6   7   8   9   10
None   Moderate   Strong
IF IMPORTANT, WHY?

ACTIVITY PAGE

RESPONSES write your Validations in the space provided below.

RECORD NOTES, Reactions, Questions, Comments, Drawings, Rubs, Samples

INCREASE AWARENESS Write responses to the activities found in Appendix H

DO POWER ACTIVITIES **Match – Resonate – Appreciate – Trust – Celebrate** *(see Appendix B).*

OPTION: arrange an onsite workshop with Dr. Cohen 1-360-378-6313

Text References are listed by number in Appendix G with online links.

LEARN MORE Master ECHN: online orientation course www.ecopsych.com/orient.html

PASS IT ON: Increase your expertise by 75%. Teach NHP to another person.

NATURAL ATTRACTION OVERVIEW: THE WEBSTRING OTHER BODY ACTIVITY

Gather a group of people in a circle with each person representing something in nature, a bird, soil, water, a tree, sunlight etc. Use a large ball of "natural attraction string" to demonstrate the connections between things in our Other Body. For example hunger attracts the bird to an insect so the string is unrolled from the "bird person" to the "insect person" who holds it. The insect is attracted to a flower and vice versa, so the string is further unrolled to the "flower person." Soon a web of natural attraction string is formed interconnecting all members of the group, including two people who represent humanity. An additional, single red ribbon connects those two people. It shows that people alone additionally connect with each other using the written or spoken story abstractions of literacy.

Gently, the group pulls back, senses, and enjoys how the natural attraction string that they share peacefully unites, supports and interconnects them and all of life. Then one strand of the web is cut signifying the pollution or loss of a species, habitat or relationship in our Other Body. Sadly, the weakening effect on all is noted. Another and another string is cut. Soon the original integrity, support and power of our Other Body is gone along with its spirit. This triggers hurt, despair and sadness as the group experiences their webstring attraction NNIAAL loves being injured and disconnected (12). They see how a false webstring-conquering red ribbon story makes them cut the strings while reasonable ECHN activities help them let themselves reconnect the web together, including people. See full details at http://www.ecopsych.com/ksanity.html#anchorwebstring (1)

> "I believe that the universe is the manifestation of its attraction to be and to grow, that all its parts are different growths and expressions of the same original attraction. They are all in attractive communication with each other and, thereby, parts of one organic whole. The whole has designed itself in humanity to register in at least fifty-four natural attraction senses. All parts of the whole are so beautiful, and are felt by me so intensely, that I am compelled to love it and to think of it as divine."
> - **Robinson Jeffers circa 1950, extended.**

VALUE INDEX My degree of attraction to the information on this page:

1	2	3	4	5	6	7	8	9	10
	None			Moderate			Strong		

IF IMPORTANT, WHY?

CHAPTER 5

OTHER BODY
CONSENT AND PERMISSION

CHAPTER 5
OTHER BODY CONSENT AND PERMISSION

11:05 AM Some students felt and expressed a strong need for a smoking and Coke Cola break that was a traditional part of their program so we recessed until 11:20. I suggested that as part the recess they might visit the natural area and ask their sense of Reason about whether smoking and Coke were good for their Other Body. If the latter was not asking them to smoke, who or what was?

11:25 AM I said to the group upon its return "Another fact to validate is that the literate one of our bodies that is not Earth is different from Earth because it knows the world through words that can become labels or stories."

"Words are a magnificent tool when they are used to protect, support and protect our Earth body. Here's how to accomplish this. You simply use your words to ask for a natural area's consent or permission to visit it before you get involved with it. This avoids you story way of life from being invasive of your other body. It makes your story attractive. For example:

Bob: What would happen if you walked past a complete stranger and into his house, opened his refrigerator door, took out his sandwich and ate it?

Eileen: He would be frightened, upset and angry. A fight might break out or the police called.

Bob: How could that disruption be avoided?

Eileen: You could first make a friendly connection with the stranger, thank him for listening, communicate your desire for food, and ask for and obtain his consent for you to enter the house and satisfy your hunger. A respectful, mutually supportive friendship might develop."

VALUE INDEX My degree of attraction to the information on this page:

1	2	3	4	5	6	7	8	9	10
None				Moderate				Strong	

IF IMPORTANT, WHY?

ACTIVITY PAGE

RESPONSES write your Validations in the space provided below.

RECORD NOTES, Reactions, Questions, Comments, Drawings, Rubs, Samples

INCREASE AWARENESS Write responses to the activities found in Appendix H

DO POWER ACTIVITIES **Match – Resonate – Appreciate – Trust – Celebrate** *(see Appendix B).*

OPTION: arrange an onsite workshop with Dr. Cohen 1-360-378-6313

Text References are listed by number in Appendix G with online links.

LEARN MORE Master ECHN: online orientation course www.ecopsych.com/orient.html

PASS IT ON: Increase your expertise by 75%. Teach NHP to another person.

THE GAINING CONSENT ACTIVITY

1. Nature enables things to build balanced relationships through natural attraction energies. Notice how you feel right now, then go to something in a natural area, your Other Body, that you like, that you find attractive. A park, backyard, aquarium, even a pet or potted plant will do. Their attractiveness is a tangible sensory connection. It invites, welcomes and consciously, feelingly connects you to them. Just like thirst naturally attracts you to water, or contact with water may make you thirsty, you are biologically built to naturally connect with the Earth community through cohesive sensations, natural "web-of-live" loves that feel good.

2. Thank your Other Body natural attraction that brings you to this area for being there for you. Thank it for safely activating a good feeling in you through this attraction connection.

3. Recognize that as part of the Earth community, justifiably, this natural area or thing desires and has a right to exist, build beneficial relationships and grow, just as you do. That's very fair, you a Lion and a fern have equal rights to life. Decide that you are going to respect its integrity by asking for its permission to visit it.

4. Because we are usually socialized to think in nature-conquering ways, silently, aloud or in writing, respectfully ask this natural area for its consent for you to be there and do this activity there. It will not give you permission to visit if you are going to injure, destroy or defame it, or if it will not be safe for you. Remember nature is completely natural attraction in action so, in nature negative relationships are not attractive; promise this area that you will treat it honorably.

5. Sense the area for 10 seconds or more in silence and respect. Be aware of negative signals from stress, discouragement or danger from it, such as thorns, bees, poison ivy, ticks, cliff faces or unpleasant memories, thoughts or feelings. If they appear, thank them for their "attractive" message to help you find more attractive ways to obtain good feeling and rewards safely.

ACTIVITY PAGE

RESPONSES write your Validations in the space provided below.

RECORD NOTES, Reactions, Questions, Comments, Drawings, Rubs, Samples

INCREASE AWARENESS Write responses to the activities found in Appendix H

DO POWER ACTIVITIES **Match – Resonate – Appreciate – Trust – Celebrate** *(see Appendix B).*

OPTION: arrange an onsite workshop with Dr. Cohen 1-360-378-6313

Text References are listed by number in Appendix G with online links.

LEARN MORE Master ECHN: online orientation course www.ecopsych.com/orient.html

PASS IT ON: Increase your expertise by 75%. Teach NHP to another person.

FOR EXAMPLE: "Our group was asked to select something attractive, sight unseen, from a bag full of miscellaneous objects. One adult woman blindly selected a piece of wood in the bag because she was attracted to its shape and smoothness when she groped and explored it by touch. But she had a negative reaction to the wood once she took it out of the bag and saw it. At first she did not know why she didn't like it when she viewed it, but in time, perhaps through her dreams, she realized it was a subconscious reaction. The wood was same shade of blue as the walls of a room where, as a child, she had been molested.

Ordinarily, during the 10 second waiting period another attraction would have appeared for her if she could have seen the color of the stick."

A. When the 10 seconds are up, note that if the area still feels attractive, or has become more attractive. If either, it has consented to your visit through a multitude of your natural senses.

B. If this part of the natural area no longer feels attractive, or is replaced by another attraction, thank it for its guidance and simply select another natural part of the area that feels attractive to you. Then repeat the gaining permission process. Do this until you find a ten second period when a safe attraction felt-sense remains for a place, color, shape, energy or other natural thing. When this occurs, you have attractive multisensory permission to visit it. In that moment, many additional natural senses are connecting and consenting.

6. As soon as you gain a natural attraction's permission to visit it, genuinely thank it for giving its consent. Note that you have made a contact or connection with your Other Body without trespassing or hurting it. Remember that you have the power to use this activity to accomplish the same good results in your relationship with the Other Earth body of any person, too.

7. Notice what value or benefit you may find from gaining consent and then *Validate* it by saying "I know it is true for me because I experienced it."

If you want to be a welcome part of your Other Body's attractive way of life, always use this activity to first gain its consent to visit it or seek its assistance.

VALUE INDEX My degree of attraction to the information on this page:

1	2	3	4	5	6	7	8	9	10
None				Moderate				Strong	

IF IMPORTANT, WHY?

ACTIVITY PAGE

RESPONSES write your Validations in the space provided below.

RECORD NOTES, Reactions, Questions, Comments, Drawings, Rubs, Samples

INCREASE AWARENESS Write responses to the activities found in Appendix H

DO POWER ACTIVITIES **Match – Resonate – Appreciate – Trust – Celebrate** *(see Appendix B)*.

OPTION: arrange an onsite workshop with Dr. Cohen 1-360-378-6313

Text References are listed by number in Appendix G with online links.

LEARN MORE Master ECHN: online orientation course www.ecopsych.com/orient.html

PASS IT ON: Increase your expertise by 75%. Teach NHP to another person.

ECHN empowers you to act from these classic observations:

"I go to nature to be soothed and healed, and to have my senses put in order."
- **John Burroughs circa 1873**

"Speak to the Earth and it will teach thee." - **The Bible, Job: 12, 7 circa 500 BC**

TAKE A THANK YOU WALK *(Optional, time and interest permitting)*

Go to an attractive natural area and ask for its consent to become involved with helping you with this activity. Thank it if it does. Find an attraction there, get its consent to approach it, walk up to it, thank it for the good feeling you may now have. Find the next attraction and repeat this process for ten minutes or more so that your attractions direct where you walk. What do you sense and feel during and at the end of the walk?

VALUE INDEX My degree of attraction to the information on this page:
1   2   3   4   5   6   7   8   9   10
None   Moderate   Strong
IF IMPORTANT, WHY?

CHAPTER 6

ZOMBINESS: THE FORMATION OF THE TOXIC TRIAD

CHAPTER 6
ZOMBINESS: THE FORMATION OF THE TOXIC TRIAD

11:40 AM The secret trespass we will next identify is the underlying source of our runaway disorders. It's like a virus that was injected into our mentality by a galaxy that decided to make us to change Planet Earth into a paid parking lot.

How can we identify what causes each of us to think and feel in the corrupt personal, social and environmental ways that produce our most challenging problems and disorders?

What is the prime short circuit that makes us be so separated from our Other Body?

What makes us rarely acknowledge that Earth is our powerfully unifying Other Body, no less treat it with the love and respect it, and therefore each of us, deserve.

ECHN empowers you to act from this classic observation:

> "The natural world is the larger sacred community to which we belong. To be alienated from this community is to become destitute in all that makes us human. To damage this community is to diminish our own existence. - **Thomas Berry circa 1985**

THE TROPICMAKING ADDICTION

By *validating* the truth of my experiences in and with nature for 78 years (1) I sense that when humanity moved from its tropical origins into different and cooler climates it encountered less dependable and different food and temperature conditions. It became critically important to encourage and applaud ways of thinking and feeling that, for survival, could produce more advanced tools to help our ancestors cope with these new and challenging places.

What our ancestors did is produce a mental outlook that controlled and changed our exposure to our differently supportive Other Body environment. Its colder climates were replaced by artificial, more stable and supportive warm indoor areas and techniques that mimicked the tropics.

ACTIVITY PAGE

RESPONSES write your Validations in the space provided below.

RECORD NOTES, Reactions, Questions, Comments, Drawings, Rubs, Samples

INCREASE AWARENESS Write responses to the activities found in Appendix H

DO POWER ACTIVITIES **Match – Resonate – Appreciate – Trust – Celebrate** *(see Appendix B).*

OPTION: arrange an onsite workshop with Dr. Cohen 1-360-378-6313

Text References are listed by number in Appendix G with online links.

LEARN MORE Master ECHN: online orientation course www.ecopsych.com/orient.html

PASS IT ON: Increase your expertise by 75%. Teach NHP to another person.

The demands of agriculture replaced sensing seasonal, less reliable food sources.

Heated indoor living and warmer clothing protected us from frigid temperatures and other dangers. This discouraged evolutionary biological changes in us, as in others, that would enable us to adapt naturally instead of artificially.

Technologies enhanced and strengthened our natural abilities so we became more able to do most anything using tools to produce substitutes for natural areas and sensibilities.

Our real-time contact with our Other Body became indoor contact time with artificial and abstract stories for over 95 percent of our lives, on average.

Thinking and feeling that was in tune with our Other Body, on average, took place for less than twelve hours per lifetime for each individual.

We omitted paying attention to our Other Body signals. Our Other Body signaled any specific technology or story was going too far and was out of balance. This was the natural NNIAAL homeostasis that kept the dance of our Other Body pure and in equilibrium with optimums for all. Today, experiencing NNIAAL helps us transform our excessiveness into mutually beneficial support.

THE TRIAD DELUSION

Our ancestor's powerful changes towards producing greater artificiality were mainly achieved by three senses, **Consciousness, Reason and Language** (CRL). They became a rewarded, but also an Other Body, isolated and linked-to-each-other, story-bonded "Triad," dedicated to survival by giving directions and manipulation. CRL was an addiction to being different than Nature and Earh because CRL was and remains bonded to be Literate. It is a mediation, not the real thing, not our non-literate Other Body.

The Triad was applauded for creating stories that were blue prints for how to manage, conquer or exploit our Other Body and create, instead, more human-comfortable, nature-disconnected, indoor, tropic-like ways to survive. The better the Triad accomplished this,

VALUE INDEX My degree of attraction to the information on this page:

1   2   3   4   5   6   7   8   9   10
      None   Moderate   Strong
IF IMPORTANT, WHY?

ACTIVITY PAGE

RESPONSES write your Validations in the space provided below.

RECORD NOTES, Reactions, Questions, Comments, Drawings, Rubs, Samples

INCREASE AWARENESS Write responses to the activities found in Appendix H

DO POWER ACTIVITIES **Match – Resonate – Appreciate – Trust – Celebrate** *(see Appendix B)*.

OPTION: arrange an onsite workshop with Dr. Cohen 1-360-378-6313

Text References are listed by number in Appendix G with online links.

LEARN MORE Master ECHN: online orientation course www.ecopsych.com/orient.html

PASS IT ON: Increase your expertise by 75%. Teach NHP to another person.

the more it was rewarded while it buried natural homeostasis and its balancing powers. This factor became a welcome, but misled, isolated, 'be-wilderment' (wilderness-separation), nature-conquering energy. With its continued acclaim, it hallucinated itself into the delusion that humanity was "the most intelligent species on Earth," and the circulation of money that the Triad invented could replace the natural circulation of pure water, air and energy.

The clearly stated, artificial, tropic-imitating non-organic story of our central scientific and religious thinking today is still to conquer, subdue and control nature, our organic planet body. In the name of success, progress and economic growth we educate ourselves to do this so aggressively that we can't control it, even when we want to. It controls us. That's a way to define addiction and prejudice but we seldom address it as such.

ECHN empowers you to act from this classic observation:

> "I fear the day when the technology overlaps with our humanity. The world will only have a generation of idiots." - **Albert Einstein circa 1939**

TRIAD SENSORY DEPRIVATION

The Triad, missing the wise and fulfilling sensory contact and support from our Other Body, suffers its loss. For this reason it has a strong and continual need for immediate gratification from artifacts, money, power and prestige, even while the detrimental consequences of them to our Other Body are in full view and growing.

From each reward it receives, the addiction of the CRL Triad to its wayward and unchecked Tropicmaking ways becomes stronger and the rut we are each in deepens (15). This is corrupt stupidity. Our sense of Reason can't think sanely. Emotionally attached and locked into the nature-conquering Triad, it is isolated, deprived, short-circuited and runaway yet we continue to reward it for its bonded consciousness to the destructive story of excessively conquering nature while not knowing how to stop.

The Triad *addiction to Literacy* makes it deaf to the sensory and reasonable pleadings of our injured Other Body and its 51 additional non-literate, natural attraction senses. Without the

ACTIVITY PAGE

RESPONSES write your Validations in the space provided below.

RECORD NOTES, Reactions, Questions, Comments, Drawings, Rubs, Samples

INCREASE AWARENESS Write responses to the activities found in Appendix H

DO POWER ACTIVITIES **Match – Resonate – Appreciate – Trust – Celebrate** *(see Appendix B).*

OPTION: arrange an onsite workshop with Dr. Cohen 1-360-378-6313

Text References are listed by number in Appendix G with online links.

LEARN MORE Master ECHN: online orientation course www.ecopsych.com/orient.html

PASS IT ON: Increase your expertise by 75%. Teach NHP to another person.

balancing and re-bonding influence of these rewarding senses on the Triad, the outcomes are disastrous.

ECHN empowers you to act from this classic observation:

> "From the moment of birth or before, when the stone-age baby first meets its twentieth-century mother, the baby is subjected to our outrageous and long existing disconnections, distortions, needs and violence of natural life including the baby's life. By the time the new human being is fifteen or so, we are left with a being like ourselves, a half-crazed creature, more or less adjusted to a mad world. This is normality in our present age." **- R. D. Laing (extended) circa 1955**

THE ZOMBINESS SYNDROME

The CRL Triad has become a self-bonded and prejudiced, nature-exploitive toxin that I call Zombiness. It is a Zombie because it is sensitivity dead to our Other Body. **Zombiness is the bound-together, emotional attachment of the senses of Consciousness, Reason and Language (CRL).** I repeat, it is a literate, but toxic Triad whose dependency on word abstracts isolates it from our sensory, non-literate Other Body, until corrected.

As a sensory Zombie the Triad is the core of "*Zombiness.*" Its self-attachment bonds of the three senses are the point source of our toxic desensitization to our Other Body, in and around us.

Our sense of Literacy in the Triad *has learned and bonded to the story* that it is necessary to disrespect Earth's natural attraction callings and make them half-truth words for the cause of "Tropicmaking Survival." This has gone far past our needs for survival. However, it won't stop because it's addicted to the artificial rewards it manufactures, often no matter the outcomes and negative effects. This is like a carrot hanging in front of a horse from a stick that

VALUE INDEX My degree of attraction to the information on this page:

1	2	3	4	5	6	7	8	9	10
	None			Moderate				Strong	

IF IMPORTANT, WHY?

ACTIVITY PAGE

RESPONSES write your Validations in the space provided below.

RECORD NOTES, Reactions, Questions, Comments, Drawings, Rubs, Samples

INCREASE AWARENESS Write responses to the activities found in Appendix H

DO POWER ACTIVITIES **Match – Resonate – Appreciate – Trust – Celebrate** *(see Appendix B).*

OPTION: arrange an onsite workshop with Dr. Cohen 1-360-378-6313

Text References are listed by number in Appendix G with online links.

LEARN MORE Master ECHN: online orientation course www.ecopsych.com/orient.html

PASS IT ON: Increase your expertise by 75%. Teach NHP to another person.

is attached to and moves with the horse.

Connecting our toxic Zombiness with the full organic renewing, purifying and recycling powers our Other Body in natural areas enables us to address this horse and carrot problem. There we can create moments that let Earth itself, our Other Body, teach us what we need to know while providing our Zombiness with unifying Natural Attraction sensory rewards instead of artificial ones. The art and science of Educating, Counseling and Healing With Nature (ECHN) makes it possible for us to achieve this (8).

By enabling us to repeatedly create moments that let Earth speak and Validate them, ECHN helps us align, embrace and transform our Zombiness into mutually supportive relationships with our Other Body. ECHN accomplishes this by helping us re-connect and interlace our CRL Triad with the powerful and rewarding Natural Attraction healing and recycling ways of our Other Body, in and around us as well as Validate it. Validating helps us remove the short circuit in our mind. It involves CRL, NNIAAL and our Other Body in registering the truth of more reasonable information and experiences.

THE ZOMBINESS JUGGERNAUT

When we are deprived, we want, and when we want there is never enough. This makes our uncorrected Zombiness a runaway addiction to attain ever-increasing perks from additional artificialities, money, prestige and power. It does this in excessive ways and quantities that assault our Other Body. Today, we take 150 percent more from our Other Body than it can give. Is it any wonder that we feel wounded and the environment is deteriorating? Is it any wonder that we fear death excessively when we sense and feel that our Other Body life support system is being destroyed?

In Industrial Society, we learn and sense from birth on, that our overpowering Zombiness is the part of every person's psyche that is intelligently in charge of how to think and feel.

Society indoctrinates our personal Consciousness, Reason and Language (CRL) Triad to become toxic, to make our pure Earth body become our polluted and excessively artificial

VALUE INDEX My degree of attraction to the information on this page:

1	2	3	4	5	6	7	8	9	10
	None				Moderate			Strong	

IF IMPORTANT, WHY?

ACTIVITY PAGE

RESPONSES write your Validations in the space provided below.

RECORD NOTES, Reactions, Questions, Comments, Drawings, Rubs, Samples

INCREASE AWARENESS Write responses to the activities found in Appendix H

DO POWER ACTIVITIES **Match – Resonate – Appreciate – Trust – Celebrate** *(see Appendix B).*

OPTION: arrange an onsite workshop with Dr. Cohen 1-360-378-6313

Text References are listed by number in Appendix G with online links.

LEARN MORE Master ECHN: online orientation course www.ecopsych.com/orient.html

PASS IT ON: Increase your expertise by 75%. Teach NHP to another person.

Industrial world. The latter is presently a juggernaut, a society that greedily goads us, for profit and status, into cravings for things and relationships that far exceed what we need to reasonably enjoy survival in balance. It then economically profits excessively Zombified individuals to sell these things and relationships to us. For example: thinking and feeling that we are not good enough unless we wear matching cell phone colors and clothing, or that we own a Rolex Watch, are far from being survival necessities. Trophy animal heads on our wall do not contribute to living sustainably. Rich and poor alike feeling that they need 15 percent more income makes no sense and is a symptom of our nature-deficient, wanting madness.

ECHN empowers you to act from this classic observation:

> "My name is Chellis, and I am in recovery from Western Civilization"
> **- Chellis Glendinning author, 1994**

Our Zombiness juggernaut will continue to damage our Other Body until we treat Zombiness as a dangerous addiction and learn how to transform its bonded ways into thinking and feeling that rewards us and it with balanced happiness, in and around us. Our ability to accomplish this is available. The sensory Natural Attraction Ecology activities of ECHN attach our psyche to the self-correcting, restorative and purifying powers of our Other Body, backyard or backcountry. This provides enlightened fulfillment for those who do it.

ECHN's organic form of psychology enables us to enjoy an emotionally supportive familiarity with our wonderful Other Body rather than continue to hurt ourselves and each other with the corrupt and destructive prejudice of our Zombiness against it."

We have developed amazing scientific stories that help us produce superb technologies like the automobile. However misleading stories intoxicate us so we don't drive the car sanely. Sadly, it becomes "normal" for us to collide with and injure our Other Body.

ECHN gives us the scientific means to stop our "untrained driver" madness. It is a sensory social technology that enables us to genuinely connect with the wisdom of our Other Body and learn to drive with its expertise, balance and beauty.

VALUE INDEX My degree of attraction to the information on this page:

1   2   3   4   5   6   7   8   9   10
None   Moderate   Strong
IF IMPORTANT, WHY?

ACTIVITY PAGE

RESPONSES write your Validations in the space provided below.

RECORD NOTES, Reactions, Questions, Comments, Drawings, Rubs, Samples

INCREASE AWARENESS Write responses to the activities found in Appendix H

DO POWER ACTIVITIES **Match – Resonate – Appreciate – Trust – Celebrate** *(see Appendix B)*.

OPTION: arrange an onsite workshop with Dr. Cohen 1-360-378-6313

Text References are listed by number in Appendix G with online links.

LEARN MORE Master ECHN: online orientation course www.ecopsych.com/orient.html

PASS IT ON: Increase your expertise by 75%. Teach NHP to another person.

11:50 AM I say to the group, "When you have the opportunity, sit quietly in a small natural area near a shopping mall for a while. There, encourage your Other Body to signal to you its sensory reactions to both of them from what I have shared, above. If you experience something passionate that makes sense *Validate.* Your passion energy will rewardingly urge your senses of reason and consciousness to be more sensible and use the process of ECHN to un-bond from the destructive story and bonding of our Zombiness that you may locate. Doing this enables you to supportively depend upon ECHN to help you anytime become healthier and happier by re-bonding to the balancing natural attraction wisdom of your other body, Earth, as of old (9). If this feels right to you, *Validate.*

On my National Audubon Society expedition education programs we would do 16 hour solos on wild islands and then the same in a shopping mall. We experienced renewal on the islands and headaches in the mall."

SUMMARY VALIDATION

12:10 PM "Now we are going to put together all the personal truths we have discovered this morning and use that collection to help us remedy our disorders, " I said. "But first, let's see who can't validate a summary of how the science of ECHN works. Will everybody here raise one hand and only put it down when you hear something in this one-minute summary that does not make sense to you. Ready?" When they all had their hands up, I slowly read aloud to them:

'To achieve greater sensibility, health and happiness we can use the process of ECHN to stop our addiction to the destructive, nature-conquering CRL story that makes our Zombiness exploit and injure our other body, Earth, in and around us.

ECHN works because it enables us create reasonable sensory moments in natural areas,

VALUE INDEX My degree of attraction to the information on this page:

1	2	3	4	5	6	7	8	9	10
None				Moderate			Strong		

IF IMPORTANT, WHY?

ACTIVITY PAGE

RESPONSES write your Validations in the space provided below.

RECORD NOTES, Reactions, Questions, Comments, Drawings, Rubs, Samples

INCREASE AWARENESS Write responses to the activities found in Appendix H

DO POWER ACTIVITIES **Match – Resonate – Appreciate – Trust – Celebrate** *(see Appendix B).*

OPTION: arrange an onsite workshop with Dr. Cohen 1-360-378-6313

Text References are listed by number in Appendix G with online links.

LEARN MORE Master ECHN: online orientation course www.ecopsych.com/orient.html

PASS IT ON: Increase your expertise by 75%. Teach NHP to another person.

backyard or backcountry, that let us connect with and benefit from the restorative and purifying powers of our Other Body while helping others learn to do the same.

The ECHN Warranty guarantees that in any given moment ECHN gives our thoughts and feelings clear access to our Other Body as a source of higher power because we are using higher power whenever we are attracted to connect with it."

All the hands had remained up, so I said, "Let's make a written copy of this summary and whenever it feels right to you *Validate* it. The more you repeat doing this, the better Nature will work for you as your higher power."

* * *

12:15 PM "It's just before our lunch break, and I'm going to describe and summarize what the truths that we discovered today show us about why and how you ended up in jail.

We are all born from and supported by our Other Body. However, from womb to tomb we learn and are victimized by becoming addicted to our CRL Zombiness story that demeans or omits our Other Body from our thinking and feeling while conquering it for profit and power. The "disconnection" story both surrounds us and is in us as it invades our thoughts and feelings. It captures and jails our senses of Reason, Literacy and Consciousness. (*See Appendix C for details*).

Our not being given believable words to know or describe our Other Body makes the 54 senses, sensitivities and sensibilities it consists of subconscious. Like the air, our Other Body is there for us but due to our veil of disconnected literacy/stories, it is hidden so we can't see it.

REACTING TO BODILY ASSAULT

Our Zombiness in its hurtful exploitation of Earth hurts our Other Body and our story way of knowing, and the two combined are who we are. This occurs especially when we are children for then we are defenseless against the story world. For example, as a kid I was unaccepted, demeaned and manipulated at school because my Other Body was left-handed. This

ACTIVITY PAGE

RESPONSES write your Validations in the space provided below.

RECORD NOTES, Reactions, Questions, Comments, Drawings, Rubs, Samples

INCREASE AWARENESS Write responses to the activities found in Appendix H

DO POWER ACTIVITIES **Match – Resonate – Appreciate – Trust – Celebrate** *(see Appendix B).*

OPTION: arrange an onsite workshop with Dr. Cohen 1-360-378-6313

Text References are listed by number in Appendix G with online links.

LEARN MORE Master ECHN: online orientation course www.ecopsych.com/orient.html

PASS IT ON: Increase your expertise by 75%. Teach NHP to another person.

rejection injured me and many disorders began to appear: finger nail biting, speech defects, unexplained muscle cramps, posture changes and tantrums, to name a few. Even now, just by just thinking about this, I have triggered and feel that pain from 77 years ago. Our Other Body seldom forgets hurtful trespasses against it, even when it buries them out of our habitual level of consciousness. The discomfort makes us act in unreasonable ways because we have to prevent it from coming into consciousness or subdue it. We seem out of touch with reality because reality is *Now*, and we bring into it and react mostly to imaginary stories of the past or future, from different times and places. This is a good description of madness.

You have shared today how many of our Zombiness ways of politics and business injured you. Your Other Body rebelled by learning to give right answers that seemed wrong and by doing uncomfortable things you were forced to do. This moved you to feel uneasy or angry, to steal, lie, manipulate and run away, hide, isolate, drink, drug, fight, associate with people you didn't like, do things you promised yourself you would never do, keep secrets that damaged your ability to celebrate your Other Body, make habits and lifestyles out of denying your authenticity, and sacrifice play, trust, love and pure joy.

Via its discomfort, our Other Body knows that it has been trespassed or invaded by our Zombiness. Your personal wholeness often recognizes this as a form of rape and, in response, it passionately and protectively helps you identify and cope with or escape the rapist. For this reason you can get some satisfaction by identifying our society's Zombiness as a sick, insensitive fucker that has screwed you since childhood and that continues to rape you today because you don't know how to stop it. It certainly has never sought your consent for what it is doing, nor have you given it consent. Anything that triggers this feeling is experienced as a fucker because it scrapes our injured Other Body.

Are you aware that you curse because it feels good to release anger over something or someone that seems to be fucking you over and/or once did? Or, you may feel that our Zombiness, in and about you, is a desensitized shit head that treats you like excrement because that's how its Zombiness experiences have been and are treating it.

You have every right to passionately curse Zombiness, to speak your heart and release the pain of your hurt, wordless, defenseless Other Body. That feeling is your natural senses 25-27

ACTIVITY PAGE

RESPONSES write your Validations in the space provided below.

RECORD NOTES, Reactions, Questions, Comments, Drawings, Rubs, Samples

INCREASE AWARENESS Write responses to the activities found in Appendix H

DO POWER ACTIVITIES **Match – Resonate – Appreciate – Trust – Celebrate** *(see Appendix B)*.

OPTION: arrange an onsite workshop with Dr. Cohen 1-360-378-6313

Text References are listed by number in Appendix G with online links.

LEARN MORE Master ECHN: online orientation course www.ecopsych.com/orient.html

PASS IT ON: Increase your expertise by 75%. Teach NHP to another person.

signaling you that you are in danger and for you to find some additional natural attractions for fulfillment and protection.

To stop you from stopping it, Zombiness makes itself look good and tries to further control you by demeaning you for using foul language. 'Well Fuck that!' you can say to yourself, or to friends who understand. You can cry to release your sadness and pain, too. However, just be proud that you are sensible enough to see, feel and want to stop the madness of the assault on your Other Body. Do whatever it is safe to do to ward off the Zombiness juggernaut before it annihilates your soul and the fullness of life on Earth.

Our Zombiness, today, will go to no ends to guard itself from experiencing its shame for having been made stupid by the Zombiness that invaded it during its childhood. Deep down it knows that it is short-circuited reasoning and feeling that is guilty of a crime against its and your Other Body. It's not your fault. Zombiness is guilty for making you what you have become and what you are being punished for. This is the devastating history of Industrial Society. It is why our society can't stop doing stupid things, even when it wants to. It suffers from the corrupt, bonded, 3-sense CRL addiction of our Zombiness that desperately needs to transform by plugging into to our Other Body, in and around us.

DEALING WITH ADDICTION

Have you noticed how introducing new, better, reasoning, consciousness or stories seldom makes a change in Zombiness unless consistent levels of rewards and/or punishments accompany these stories? Story changes alone don't make change in addiction? We must in addition release our CRL bonds to old ways and stories, by providing greater rewards from the new ways (including the reward of stopping a punishment after it has started). ECHN is a process that helps our Other Body provide reasonable, attraction-based rewards from our Other Body contact.

Today, ECHN provides you with the ability to bring into play our Other Body's planet-strong, refreshing, psyche-recycling preventatives and mind-composting remedies for our runaway

VALUE INDEX My degree of attraction to the information on this page:

1	2	3	4	5	6	7	8	9	10
None				Moderate				Strong	

IF IMPORTANT, WHY?

ACTIVITY PAGE

RESPONSES write your Validations in the space provided below.

RECORD NOTES, Reactions, Questions, Comments, Drawings, Rubs, Samples

INCREASE AWARENESS Write responses to the activities found in Appendix H

DO POWER ACTIVITIES **Match – Resonate – Appreciate – Trust – Celebrate** *(see Appendix B).*

OPTION: arrange an onsite workshop with Dr. Cohen 1-360-378-6313

Text References are listed by number in Appendix G with online links.

LEARN MORE Master ECHN: online orientation course www.ecopsych.com/orient.html

PASS IT ON: Increase your expertise by 75%. Teach NHP to another person.

Zombiness corruption. You need every bit of energy and help that you can find if you are going to win your battle for your sanity and safety against the mind pollution caused by Zombiness. Remember that Zombiness surrounds you and is in you. Its toxic stories have invaded, polluted or raped the way you and your Other Body inherently think and feel in attractive balance. We are all in recovery from our "socialized normalcy."

ECHN empowers you to act from this classic observation:

> "The interior landscape responds to the character and subtlety of the exterior landscape; the shape of the individual mind is affected by the land as it is by genes."
> - **Barry Lopez circa 1987**

The significant contribution that identifying Zombiness makes is that it helps each of us recognize that the point source of our disorders and problems is the Zombiness that lies in ourselves and others. It is not another individual or group or ourselves that causes problems, it is the Zombiness CRL Bonds in and around us and them that have crippled or corrupted all of us from stopping addiction. It's the destructive bonds that need the correction of being un-bonded from Other Body disconnection stories and rebounded to how to reconnect.

The challenge for each of us is to remedy problems by using ECHN activities to help us help others and ourselves make genuine sensory contact with the higher power of our Other Body in natural areas, backyard or backcountry as well as in each other. Doing this gives our Other Body the time, space and energy to un-bond and healthfully re-bond our destructive Zombiness to organic stories. It rewardingly enables our CRL Triad stories and addictions to change, to transform as moment by moment we choose to make reasonable connections to the purifying and healing powers of our Other Body in people and places. This is helping folks reasonably, rather than just punishing folks who need help.

ECHN empowers you to act from this classic observation:

> "We are not ourselves when nature, being oppressed, commands the mind to suffer with the body." - **William Shakespeare circa 1590**

VALUE INDEX My degree of attraction to the information on this page:

1	2	3	4	5	6	7	8	9	10
	None			Moderate			Strong		

IF IMPORTANT, WHY?

ACTIVITY PAGE

RESPONSES write your Validations in the space provided below.

RECORD NOTES, Reactions, Questions, Comments, Drawings, Rubs, Samples

INCREASE AWARENESS Write responses to the activities found in Appendix H

DO POWER ACTIVITIES **Match – Resonate – Appreciate – Trust – Celebrate** *(see Appendix B)*.

OPTION: arrange an onsite workshop with Dr. Cohen 1-360-378-6313

Text References are listed by number in Appendix G with online links.

LEARN MORE Master ECHN: online orientation course www.ecopsych.com/orient.html

PASS IT ON: Increase your expertise by 75%. Teach NHP to another person.

* * *

Again do the recovery experiment on your trip to the Lunch Room, now. Take the path there that goes through a natural area and have your sense of reason make your sense of literacy repeatedly label every natural attraction it sees as 'Nameless,' 'Attraction,' 'Subconscious,' 'Unity,' or 'Other Body.' Experiment. Note what changes may take place in what you sense and feel each of these Other Body descriptions. Which one works best for you, which is most attractive to you? Do they help you recognize or deal with you Zombiness? For me, everything becomes more vibrant and brighter when I do this. I sense that I am welcome and supported in this speechless other family of mine. I hear things I was missing. It feels wonderful, like a trip through an enchanted forest that embraces me and clears my mind. I am told it is like I am tripping but in a good way, a way whose effects make sense, a way that does not produce hurtful side effects or addiction. The satisfactions we gain from eating organic food are the same thing. What happens for you?"

One Participant said:

"In each case, once the words were removed or made to accurately label the natural area as attraction or nameless, everything became brighter or more intense. Sounds came into my awareness that were missing up to that time, including the swish of my feet through the grass and the whisper of my breathing. A heightened sense of aliveness came into play that was stress-less and calming, almost like a dream to which I was very attentive. It was a lovely 'vacation' from ordinary thinking. The thing that felt most attractive was seeing other people engaged in the activity from this four-leg state of consciousness."

ECHN empowers you to act from this classic observation:

> "The beginning of wisdom is to call things by their right name."
> - **Confucius circa 500 B.C**

* * *

ACTIVITY PAGE

RESPONSES write your Validations in the space provided below.

RECORD NOTES, Reactions, Questions, Comments, Drawings, Rubs, Samples

INCREASE AWARENESS Write responses to the activities found in Appendix H

DO POWER ACTIVITIES **Match – Resonate – Appreciate – Trust – Celebrate** *(see Appendix B).*

OPTION: arrange an onsite workshop with Dr. Cohen 1-360-378-6313

Text References are listed by number in Appendix G with online links.

LEARN MORE Master ECHN: online orientation course www.ecopsych.com/orient.html

PASS IT ON: Increase your expertise by 75%. Teach NHP to another person.

LUNCH BREAK

1:30 PM When we gathered after lunch I invited group members to share what happened when they did the walk to lunch and which word or word combinations worked best for them. For each who did share we validated. It was good to see some participants encouraging others to share and help Validate each others' attractions. We do this because, as we have already validated, natural attraction as NNIAAL is the essence of how our Other Body maintains its beauty, purity and balance, from atomic particles to galaxies and beyond. As we help it recover in others, we help it recover in ourselves.

We concluded that:

Seeking higher power in nature via ECHN enables our Other Body to compost and recycle our Zombiness. Well-being, happiness and wholeness results in and around us.

We build healthy and more trustable friendships by carefully seeking and supporting our Other Body that we can sense and feel in another person.

If the United Nations insisted that all UN meetings along with the governmental meetings of each nation start with all the delegates being ECHN literate enough to do the "Gaining Consent from our Other Body activity (Chapter 5), we could stamp out Zombiness and its destructive effects in a generation.

ECHN empowers you to act from these classic observations:

> "Corruption is authority plus monopoly minus transparency"- **Author Unknown**

> "Truth is rarely writ in ink; it lives in nature."- **Martin H. Fischer Circa 1950**

> "Many of us came to tears when we as strangers walked around outdoors in a tight ellipse that had all of us face each other one-on-one, hold hands for five seconds and say 'I love you as of old,' and then move on."- **Helen Waite Circa 1981**

VALUE INDEX My degree of attraction to the information on this page:

1	2	3	4	5	6	7	8	9	10
	None				Moderate			Strong	

IF IMPORTANT, WHY?

CHAPTER 7

I LOVE MY OTHER BODY

CHAPTER 7
I LOVE MY OTHER BODY

1:52 PM "We are now going to do a Zombiness remedy activity. It gives us an opportunity to make our sense of literacy story-telling powers help us make strong attraction contact with our non-literate Other Body, recognizing that our Other Body only understands natural attraction because that's all it is.

1. Find an attractive moment of your Other Body in a natural area. It could be a park, a plant, a pet, a stone, a stream, a tree, a backyard, a view, a cloud, a birdsong, a mountain, a meadow.

Use the consent activity we have already practiced (Chapter 5) to gain permission from the natural area to visit it and do an activity with it. After you gain its consent,

2. Spend a few moments discovering what it is here that attracts you. When you are comfortable feeling attracted to whatever it is that attracts you, write the following and fill in the blanks:

I love this_____ because it_____.

An example: 'I love (am attracted to, or like) this rock *because it is enduring and warm*.' Write down or remember what you have said in your attraction statement.

Repeat the above with another attraction if time and attraction permit.

3. Return to the group being prepared to share your statement

4. When the group convenes share your statement and help others share their statements. *Validate*

5. Now, take your "I love" sentence that you saved and in the first blank and substitute "myself," for the nature attraction. Then complete the sentence with the words you selected for your appreciation of your Other Body.

ACTIVITY PAGE

RESPONSES write your Validations in the space provided below.

RECORD NOTES, Reactions, Questions, Comments, Drawings, Rubs, Samples

INCREASE AWARENESS Write responses to the activities found in Appendix H

DO POWER ACTIVITIES **Match – Resonate – Appreciate – Trust – Celebrate** *(see Appendix B)*.

OPTION: arrange an onsite workshop with Dr. Cohen 1-360-378-6313

Text References are listed by number in Appendix G with online links.

LEARN MORE Master ECHN: online orientation course www.ecopsych.com/orient.html

PASS IT ON: Increase your expertise by 75%. Teach NHP to another person.

For example: I like (or love) this rock because it is enduring and warm.

becomes: I like (or love) myself because I am enduring and warm."

Read your new sentence aloud a few times. How does it feel? Do you sense a moment of meaning that strengthens your relationship with yourself and your Other Body? When you can acknowledge that it is a truth about you and your Other Body, express how that feels.

Then *Validate* the statement and the feeling.

Your revised sentence "tricks" your nature disconnected awareness to become more conscious of Literate You *plus* your Other Body. You sense, feel and know your total self and its value. Because this is attractive and makes sense to your wholeness, it can make you feel good.

Can you validate that the changed sentence: "I like (or love) myself because (2)_____" describes some natural aspect of your totality, your Whole Self. How do you feel about yourself in this light? Does it feel right? Feel good? *Validate*

You can be absolutely sure that some part of you is described by this sentence because it is that part of you that discovered and had the ability to register the part of your Other Body that you found attractive in the first section of the activity. This is an important, full disclosure, self-worth discovery, an inventory of our relationship with our Other Body.

ECHN empowers you to act from this classic observation:

> "What we are looking for is what is looking." - **St. Francis of Assisi circa 1210**

A Participant's Reaction

"I love this dead branch that has fallen off the tree because it holds the rain and is supporting the life of the moss and other things growing from it. I love myself because I am a dead branch that has fallen off the tree and I am holding the rain and supporting the life of the

ACTIVITY PAGE

RESPONSES write your Validations in the space provided below.

RECORD NOTES, Reactions, Questions, Comments, Drawings, Rubs, Samples

INCREASE AWARENESS Write responses to the activities found in Appendix H

DO POWER ACTIVITIES **Match – Resonate – Appreciate – Trust – Celebrate** *(see Appendix B)*.

OPTION: arrange an onsite workshop with Dr. Cohen 1-360-378-6313

Text References are listed by number in Appendix G with online links.

LEARN MORE Master ECHN: online orientation course www.ecopsych.com/orient.html

PASS IT ON: Increase your expertise by 75%. Teach NHP to another person.

moss and other things growing from me."

"How does that feel, what do you think?"

"Its saying that part of me feels dead because I'm in prison here but because I'm holding to my Other Body for life I'm helping others grow....so this shows I'm still alive as my Other Body and I'm helping it and me grow. "

I said, "I apologize that my words misled you a little bit to help your Toxic Triad Zombiness know and value your Other Body more fully so it might change its toxic story a bit. However, now that you know this activity, you can always use it as a special tool to trick the Toxic Triad in and around you so you may discover, nourish and celebrate subconscious hidden parts of yourself. They will sneakily weaken the Toxic Triad and make your wholeness stronger. All you need to do is make honest "like" or "love" statements about natural attractions you find, and this includes those you find in the Other Body of other people, too. These loves can strengthen your relationships with others, especially if you do this activity together and share the results.

If reading the 'I love myself because' sentence makes you feel uncomfortable, search your life for at least one incident, example or dream relating to the sentence that feels right or accurate. Perhaps you can imagine or create one, if necessary. You might ask others in the group to help you find this part of yourself. Friends usually can see past your self-doubts.

Your sentence may be a metaphor. Try to find examples of parts of yourself that accurately match this metaphor. Remember that sometimes you have been taught to deny them, because they are your Other Body, and, in our nature-separated society, like a weed, our Other Body is usually removed, not supported. For this reason, many people have trouble admitting shamelessly they are naturally beautiful, strong, worthy, etc. and this erodes their self-worth and their ability to choose as the united and intact wholeness of two bodies and/or all bodies as part of the Standard Universe.

VALUE INDEX My degree of attraction to the information on this page:
1   2   3   4   5   6   7   8   9   10
None   Moderate   Strong
IF IMPORTANT, WHY?

ACTIVITY PAGE

RESPONSES write your Validations in the space provided below.

RECORD NOTES, Reactions, Questions, Comments, Drawings, Rubs, Samples

INCREASE AWARENESS Write responses to the activities found in Appendix H

DO POWER ACTIVITIES **Match – Resonate – Appreciate – Trust – Celebrate** *(see Appendix B)*.

OPTION: arrange an onsite workshop with Dr. Cohen 1-360-378-6313

Text References are listed by number in Appendix G with online links.

LEARN MORE Master ECHN: online orientation course www.ecopsych.com/orient.html

PASS IT ON: Increase your expertise by 75%. Teach NHP to another person.

6. When others in the group complete 5, above, help them find, express and *Validate* their experience."

* * *

When I did the activity with the group I was attracted and gained consent to visit a straight-line of tall, dark trees that welcomed me as if they were a protective fence for me. They were silhouetted against a tan background and that caught my interest because the rest of the countryside around me was dark green mountainsides, not tan. I was attracted to get closer only to discover the "Tan" was a clear-cut side of a mountain where all the trees had been removed or pulverized into wood chips. I walked into the clear-cut. Its baron atmosphere of death triggered feelings of alarm, regret and loss of friends or community

"I love these trees because they are protectively alerting or warning me, like a guard rail, to the fact that Other Body dancers like them and me have been cut down or ground up into wood chips."

This became:

"I love myself because I care for me like a protective fence and I alert myself to the fact that others and parts of me have been cut down or ground up and converted into the baron and hurtful ways of industrial society"

When I shared this experience with the group, the message was Validated and well taken. They and I thanked this outdoor recovery program and natural area for having the assault on our Other Body clearly visible in the clear cut.

ECHN empowers you to act from these classic observations:

> "And the true order of going, or being led by another, to the things of love, is to begin from the beauties of earth." - **Plato circa 400 B.C.**

> "There must be the generating force of love behind every effort that is to be successful."
> - **Henry David Thoreau circa 1845**

VALUE INDEX My degree of attraction to the information on this page:
1   2   3   4   5   6   7   8   9   10
None   Moderate   Strong
IF IMPORTANT, WHY?

ACTIVITY PAGE

RESPONSES write your Validations in the space provided below.

RECORD NOTES, Reactions, Questions, Comments, Drawings, Rubs, Samples

INCREASE AWARENESS Write responses to the activities found in Appendix H

DO POWER ACTIVITIES **Match – Resonate – Appreciate – Trust – Celebrate** *(see Appendix B).*

OPTION: arrange an onsite workshop with Dr. Cohen 1-360-378-6313

Text References are listed by number in Appendix G with online links.

LEARN MORE Master ECHN: online orientation course www.ecopsych.com/orient.html

PASS IT ON: Increase your expertise by 75%. Teach NHP to another person.

2:40 PM "Can we share here what we felt about doing this activity and how it tricked our sense of literacy into acknowledging and supporting our Other Body?

* * *

2:55 PM We have time to do a couple more activities with our Other Body that help us strengthen our relationship with it by letting it communicate with its reasonable attraction to un-addict the toxic CRL Zombiness around and within us.

Each activity, and each time you do it, further helps the Triad reduce its addiction to hurtful and false Other Body stories. The addiction is replaced by attractive true stories and emotional rewards for reasoning that include better stories and the welfare of our Other Body

3:20 PM Read through the Warranty we offer. Are their any things in it that you don't understand or would like to comment on? (*Appendix A*)

3:25 PM Does this statement help you recognize how much you have learned or need to learn? What degree of attraction score do you give for this statement?

"Seeking higher power in nature via ECHN enables our Other Body to compost Zombiness, transform it and recycle it into the happiness of wholeness."

1   2   3   4   5   6   7   8   9   10

not attractive   somewhat attractive   very attractive

3:30 PM Based on the great work you did today, you now have the understanding and means to continue on as a self-educating group using nature more and more as your Higher Power when you attracted to do so. In conjunction with your Other Body, doing this can help ourselves, and each other further transform your addictions and troubles into beneficial organic relationships by assisting each other in making more Other Body contact.   You can

VALUE INDEX My degree of attraction to the information on this page:
1   2   3   4   5   6   7   8   9   10
None   Moderate   Strong
IF IMPORTANT, WHY?

ACTIVITY PAGE

RESPONSES write your Validations in the space provided below.

RECORD NOTES, Reactions, Questions, Comments, Drawings, Rubs, Samples

INCREASE AWARENESS Write responses to the activities found in Appendix H

DO POWER ACTIVITIES **Match – Resonate – Appreciate – Trust – Celebrate** *(see Appendix B).*

OPTION: arrange an onsite workshop with Dr. Cohen 1-360-378-6313

Text References are listed by number in Appendix G with online links.

LEARN MORE Master ECHN: online orientation course www.ecopsych.com/orient.html

PASS IT ON: Increase your expertise by 75%. Teach NHP to another person.

get course credit for doing this and further training in it so you may become a coach, or a counselor, like Steve, to help others learn how to improve their lives, and all of life, by re-connecting with their Other Body. (22)

ECHN has about 160 different activities that help us re-connect and remedy a wide variety of harmful Other Body disconnections that are common in Industrial Society. The courses, certification or degree in doing this work is located at www.ecopsych.com.

ECHN empowers you to act from these classic observations:

> "In the woods we return to reason and faith. There I feel that nothing can befall me in life--no disgrace, no calamity (leaving me my eyes), which nature cannot repair. Standing on the bare ground, --my head bathed by the blithe air and uplifted into infinite space, --all mean egotism vanishes. I become a transparent eyeball; I am nothing, I see all; the currents of the Universal Being circulate through me; I am a part or particle of God." **- Ralph Waldo Emerson circa 1860**

> "Nature is the unseen intelligence that loved us into being."
> **- Elbert Hubbard circa 1895**

CONCLUSION

Eight Weeks Later: The all men's group, average age 24, has been meeting with Steve for four hours once a week. They do the readings and activities in our Orientation Course with him and share their responses, concerns and support together.

For best results, this kind of group should be meeting for ninety minutes every other day and sleeping one night minimum between activities so their dreams can help nature fill the new paths the activitity experiences make in their mind while their stories are asleep. That's the heart of nature-connected recovery, to help them build a supportive haven and life raft in their mentality that their Other Body continually nurtures.

ACTIVITY PAGE

RESPONSES write your Validations in the space provided below.

RECORD NOTES, Reactions, Questions, Comments, Drawings, Rubs, Samples

INCREASE AWARENESS Write responses to the activities found in Appendix H

DO POWER ACTIVITIES **Match – Resonate – Appreciate – Trust – Celebrate** *(see Appendix B).*

OPTION: arrange an onsite workshop with Dr. Cohen 1-360-378-6313

Text References are listed by number in Appendix G with online links.

LEARN MORE Master ECHN: online orientation course www.ecopsych.com/orient.html

PASS IT ON: Increase your expertise by 75%. Teach NHP to another person.

By continually *Validating,* the group is energizing their Other Body into their consciousness and developing a strong and firm, whole life, intelligence, an immediate sense of self and community that they can trust and rely on in themselves, others and natural areas. They benefit from our Other Body and NNIAAL being as constant, steady and secure as "zero and one" are for the foundational accuracy of mathematics. Too often we learn to forget that the ways and wisdom of the ages is the sun rising each morning, the stars being present at night and gravity binding us to the balanced lifeways our planetary home. Like our sensation of Thirst, that wisdom is a moment by moment, united, seamless continuum of the authenticity of the eons. It has demonstrated its power to remedy the distorted fables and warped misleading tales our new brain CRL too often invents and emotionally clings to for the excessive profit and destructive power it mistakingly thinks it needs over our Other Body for survival. Learning to trust the ancient unwavering anchor of the natural attraction "seed" is critical for developing our resilience against addiction and for solving our critical other problems and disorders in a unifying way.

Steve has continued to collect the *Validation* facts that the group discovered and I'm going to let some quotes from the participants speak for themselves here (with abusive language altered). You can decide if they are classic observations that have value. Their authors are obviously not well known but aren't they unheralded pioneers?

"This program completes my genuine seeking urge to be organized and connected because this process is already organized. It brings me peace when I seek my other body experience. The other kind of organized and connected is what got me in jail."

"Because this process goes to my Other Body, I sense I can trust it more than the no-body world of crime I came from. I worked really hard out there to live but the joke was on me that I was living to die, I was a nature-disconnected lie."

"This sounds and flows good, it is a fact that I get better results when I do this stuff. I feel like I'm running home every time I do these activities with you and the group. This is no bullshit, I really see the beauty, I see my beautiful other body."

"I can't believe I am in a correctional institution looking for the beauty of what I lost, this is more than crazy, but I am changing; it is a great change too, and look, I have a trustable body."

"I'm in jail and here the guards are the trees. The good soldiers are the trees that protect me from the pulverized clear-cut just across the road which was my life. Everything here has two bodies and have it in them to protect me."

"This place is like an egg hunt. I'm looking under every rock for my other body and find it every time. I'm changed for life so I cant go back to being a nobody ever again."

"I'm officially seeking to be a somebody now."

✶ ✶ ✶

As demonstrated by the information in this book the key to solving our unsolvable problems via the Webstring ECHN Model lies in the resilience and expertise of facilitators to help an individual or group, including themselves, *Validate* while being their literate Earth Body in tune with itself. To this end, a subsidized facilitator "Earth Avatar" training and degree program is available from Project NatureConnect for those who are dedicated to adding this skill to their life and/or livelihood. These folks are our future for in each of them lies a very special hope.

Contact Dr. Michael J. Cohen, nature@interisland.net, 360-378-6313, www.ecopsych.com

Summary Article: http://www.ecopsych.com/journalessence.html

APPENDICES

APPENDIX A

THE PROJECT NATURECONNECT WARRANTY
SATISFACTION GUARANTEED

Since inaccurate information can undermine the best of our thinking, feeling and relationships, Project NatureConnect (PNC) goes several steps beyond standard accreditation and other certifications. We offer this special Warranty of integrity and balance because other commonly issued assurances are seldom organic. The state of the world shows that to everybody's loss, many assurances support corrupt thoughts, feelings and acts that assault the naturally pure and self-correcting ways of the Standard Universe including our body, mind and spirit. They reinforce "normal" but destructive and distorted customs that cripple our personal, social and environmental well-being.

THE PNC ASSURANCE OF UNCORRUPTED SCIENCE, PSYCHOLOGY AND ECOLOGY INFORMATION

For those who love nature or truly care about the well-being of individuals, communities and natural areas, this Warranty affirms that your personal and professional life will significantly benefit as you make unadulterated sensory connections to authentic nature's beauty, healing and purifying powers, in and around you. We guarantee that because PNC is organic it gives you far greater wisdom and support than what is offered by the corrupt leadership, education, science, psychology, economics and spirituality that have misguided us for centuries to create the dilemmas we face and suffer today.

> "From the moment of birth or before, when the stone-age baby first meets its twentieth-century mother, the baby is subjected to our outrageous and long existing disconnections, distortions and violence of natural life including the baby's life. By the time the new human being is fifteen or so, we are left with a being like ourselves, a half-crazed creature, more or less adjusted to a mad world. This is normality in our present age." - R. D. Laing (extended) circa 1955

VALUE INDEX My degree of attraction to the information on this page:

1	2	3	4	5	6	7	8	9	10
	None				Moderate			Strong	

IF IMPORTANT, WHY?

LIFETIME WARRANTY

A Certified Organic Natural Product
I solemnly state, guarantee, bond, and warrant that the contents A-O in the affidavit, below, are correct and true.

Michael J. Cohen, Ph.D, Ed.D

Signed or Attested by Michael J. Cohen before me on 05 day of June, 2013
Signature Arlene Franco (Alias)
Printed Name Arlene Franco (Alias)
Notary Public, State of Washington, County of San Juan
My commission expires April 15, 2017

Warranty Confirmation: www.ecopsych.com/journalwarrantyconfirm.html

Project NatureConnect herein guarantees that the organic art and science of its Educating, Counseling and Healing with Nature (ECHN) process consists of credible, trustable, non-corrupt information as follows:

WHEREAS, the author of this document is a member and part of the evidence-based, historical Standard Universe (Nature), he sincerely declares and affirms that his statements, A-O, in this document are correct and true with respect to the Nature and its material, energy and spiritual components; and

WHEREAS, Nature, including humanity, is the attractive dance of the eons with the power to produce optimums of life, diversity, peace and cooperation as well as sanely organize, purify, correct, heal and balance itself and its participant dancers without producing garbage or pollution; and

WHEREAS, because central thinking and feeling in Industrial Society is, on average, over ninety-nine percent disconnected from Nature's dance in natural areas and in humanity, the citizens of Industrial Society are unable to solve the personal, social and environmental disorders that result from their excessive separation from, and undeclared war on, Nature (1); and

WHEREAS, the verified seventy-eight years of Nature-connected living and Organic Psychology research reported by myself and over three-thousand Project NatureConnect students and staff in "Educating, Counseling and Healing with Nature" (ECHN) (2) has never been disputed by valid evidence; and

WHEREAS, far beyond reasonable doubt, the facts and links presented in the Natural Attraction Ecology article "The Magic of Something From Nothing" (MSN) (3) have proven to be real; and

WHEREAS, the Natural Attraction Ecology truths (4), also found in ECHN and MSN, are based on empirical self-evidence and accuracy; and

WHEREAS, the benefits from the sensory evidence and experience gained by participating in the Natural Systems Thinking Process Web of Life Imperative (5) are rarely denied; and

WHEREAS, the favorable results reported (6) in ECHN and MSN and PeakFacts.com and its links (7) have been documented as genuine and repeatable; and

WHEREAS, creating sensory ECHN moments in time genuinely align us with Earth's self-correcting ways and teach us unadulterated truths that we need to know (8); and

WHEREAS, the ECHN process energizes into our consciousness the socially buried, but inherent, natural love and intelligence that helps us reverse our destructive prejudice against Nature and makes unparalleled contributions to personal, social and environmental well-being (9);

NOW, THEREFORE, I, Michael J. Cohen, Ph.D., the prime expedition education director, investigator and implementer of the ECHN art and science of NAE at Project NatureConnect, guarantee and warranty that the following facts are fundamental, indisputable and of critical importance in helping humanity and nature reverse Industrial Society's ongoing deterioration of personal, social and environmental well-being (10). I further warranty that it is not credible, but rather it is corrupt, unreasonable and negligent to omit or ignore these facts and their axioms as is presently common for most individuals and institutions in Industrial Society:

FACT

A. PNC is open to all qualified applicants, regardless of race, creed, color, situation, circumstance or environment, who recognize on some level that Earth is their other body and who want to learn how to relate to it in balanced ways, to the benefit of all.

B. Until proven otherwise, the energy of Natural Attraction is the attractive "unifying binding field" Higgs Boson essence of every atom, aspect and part of the Standard Universe/Nature since its Big Bang inception. This includes the thoughts, senses, feelings, intelligence and relationships of our body, mind and spirit as part of our Universe (11).

C. The Natural Attraction Dance of the Standard Universe/Nature (the Dance) only exists in the immediate moment, as do its Dancers.

D. The Dancers are all the things in our Universe, including the thoughts, senses, feelings and relationships of our body, mind and spirit. The Dancers include sensations, attractions, ideas and memories of the past, present or future along with our ability to relate to and with them (12).

E. Until fully proven otherwise, with the exception of humanity and the like, neither the Dance nor its Dancers are literate. Being non-literate and immediate, they don't have the ability to produce misleading stories or produce the destructive effects of stories that do not attractively support the Dance (13).

F. Every part of the Dance, including humanity, is in communication with the Dance in order that every individual or thing dances in attractive balance, harmony and support of the whole Dance and its Dancers, and vice versa.

G. The Dance does not produce any toxic waste. Its process of transformation into more attractive relationships enables all Dancers to belong and to be wanted; no Dancer is polluted, omitted or discarded (14).

H. When in immediate conscious sensory contact with the authentic Dance in and around us, not just stories about it, whatever an individual personally experiences is empirically true for them because, unadulterated, the experience registers directly on, and can blend with, their more than fifty-four inherent natural attraction senses and sensibilities (15). These fifty-four distinct sensations include the excessively bonded senses of Reason, Consciousness and Literacy (the Triumvirate).

I. When excessive disconnection of our body, mind or spirit from the unadulterated Dance of Nature is a cause of a problem or disorder, the process of genuinely reconnecting ourselves with the Dance is essential as part of the solution. The Dance is the fountainhead of authority in how it works. It is a remedy and preventative for nature-deficit addiction and other disorders of the Triumvirate.

J. Individuals (16) who have had a good or beneficial experience while spending quiet time in a natural area, register and are conscious on some level that the Dance, in and around us, is us and that it has attractive renewing, restorative, enchanting, corrective and purifying qualities.

K. As demonstrated by our senses registering birds, air, clouds, rain and insects in the sky above us, we each live in the Dance on Planet Earth, not in the distortion that we live on it. We are but one of its web-of-life Dancers each of whom has a right to the benefits of unadulterated life in balance (17).

L. Planet Earth is my other body. I know this is true because I feel loss, anguish and despair when I ask myself "Who would I be if somebody, or thing, took my Earth body away from me?" These feelings urge me to help others use ECHN to validate and enjoy Planet Earth as their other body and increase its, their and my well-being.

M. The validity of A-K, above, supports the truth of twenty axioms (18) that underlie the art and science of Organic Psychology and Natural Attraction Ecology.

N. No qualified individual is denied participation in the standard training, certificate and degree programs of Organic Psychology and Natural Attraction Ecology at Project NatureConnect based on their budget challenges. Because the purpose and object of PNC

VALUE INDEX My degree of attraction to the information on this page:

1	2	3	4	5	6	7	8	9	10
	None			Moderate			Strong		

IF IMPORTANT, WHY?

expedition-model education is to help people heal and support the wounded Dance, in and around themselves and others, financial assistance based on economic need is available via self-designed payment plans, work-study projects, grants, tuition subsidies, volunteerism, contributions and interest-free loans

O. This warranty is null and void if the integrity and benefits of the long established Organic Psychology/ Natural Attraction Ecology Model are adulterated by using only parts of it instead of its wholeness (2, 3, 5)

WARRANTY REFERENCES

* 1.   Cohen, M. J. 1995, Education and Counseling With Nature: A Greening of Psychotherapy. The Interspsych Newsletter, Vol 2, Issue http://www.ecopsych.com/counseling.html

* 2.   Cohen, M. J. 2008, Educating Counseling and Healing With Nature Illumina Publishing. http://www.ecopsych.com/ksanity.html

* 3.   Project NatureConnect 2012 The Magic of Something From Nothing: http://www.ecopsych.com/journalessence.html

* 4.   Project NatureConnect: Eco Zombie, Wake Up http://www.ecopsych.com/journalproof.html

* 5.   Project NatureConnect Web of Life Imperative http://www.ecopsych.com/newbook4wli.html

* 6.   Project NatureConnect, 1996, A Survey of Participants |http://www.ecopsych.com/survey.html

* 7.   Project NatureConnect Peak Fact: Whole Life Self Evidence in Action http://www.ecopsych.com/journalpeak.html

* 8.   Project NatureConnect 2007 Whom Am I? Who or What is Your Natural Self? http://www.ecopsych.com/thesisquote6.html

* 9.   Doherty, T. J. 2010, Michael Cohen: Ecopsychology Interview Ecopsychology Journal, Vol 2 No.2. Mary Jane Liebert Publishing. http://www.ecopsych.com/ecopsychologyjournal.html

* 10.   Project NatureConnect 2007 Challenge: The Considerations of a Nature-Connected Expert.
http://www.ecopsych.com/mjcohen22.html

* 11. Project NatureConnect 2000: A New Copernicun Revolution
http://www.ecopsych.com/journalcopernicus.html

* 12. Project NatureConnect 2007 Who, What or When is the Acronym NNIAAL? http://www.ecopsych.com/earthstories101.html

* 13. Project NatureConnect 2005 Thinking and Learning With all Nine Legs
http://www.ecopsych.com/nineleg.html

* 14.   Project NatureConnect 2008, How to Transform Destructive Thinking Into

Constructive Relationships.
 http://www.ecopsych.com/transformation.html
 * 15. Project NatureConnect, 1990, Connecting With Nature, World Peace University
Press
http://www.ecopsych.com/insight53senses.html
 * 16. Project NatureConnect 2007 Whom Am I? Who or What is Your Natural Self? http://
www.ecopsych.com/thesisquote6.html
 * 17. Project NatureConnect 2007, Thinking and Feeling Like the Joy of Nature
http://www.ecopsych.com/avatarpath.html
 * 18. Project NatureConnect 2007, Natural Attraction Ecology
http://www.naturalattractionecology.com/index.html#anchoraxiom

I repeat that as an Applied Ecopsychologist and Environmental Educator I solemnly state, guarantee, bond, assure and warrant that the contents A-O of this affidavit are correct and true. During periods when I sense that there is a God, I swear this oath to Him/Her/It.

Michael J. Cohen
Earth is my other body.

APPENDIX B

"SEVMRATC" ATTRACTION STRENGTHENING ACTIVITIES

After Validating the personal felt-sense, good feeling truth of natural attraction (a Sense, Enjoy and Validate (SEV) experience), you can enhance it by doing the following activities in conjunction with the attraction you have explored. Simply substitute in your attraction for the natural attraction experience found in the activities below.

Become more aware. Write in the space provided in this book, or elsewhere:
1. How and what did you feel when you had this experience?
2. The three most important things you learned from this experience?
3. How would you feel about having the experience taken away from you?
4. Did the activity enhance your sense of self-worth and your trustfulness of nature?
5. Share your reactions to the reactions of others
6. Write one or two keywords that convey what important thing you learned from this assignment.
7. Write one or more complete, single, short, power sentence "quotes" that convey a good contribution that this experience made to improving your relationships.
8. You will increase your learning from this activity by 75% if you teach this activity to another person
9. While your 5-leg mind sleeps, your 4-leg mind inhabits the inroad paths of consciousness made by this activity (8). Note, upon awakening, whether any changes have occurred with respect to your outlook or the way you feel.

Match: Once you have gone to an attractive natural area and thankfully gain its consent to do and Validate your natural attraction, Match your natural attraction. Physically assume its shape and/or motion. For example: To match the radiating shape of a leaf, posture yourself with your body and arms spread like the leaf and wave as it does in the wind. Note what you sense while doing this. This activity is similar to analytical therapies. It helps differentiate stories form the past with opportunities in the present, including the opportunity to psychologically change past stories. It helps identify injuries from the unseen war we engage in. Try to remember if or when you have felt this sensation(s) before, indoors or outdoors. It has a history throughout your life and the life of the planet. For example, you may have sensed it when you once sat in a rocking chair, climbed a tree on a windy day, or stood on a swing.

VALUE INDEX My degree of attraction to the information on this page:

1	2	3	4	5	6	7	8	9	10
None				Moderate			Strong		

IF IMPORTANT, WHY?

Ask yourself: When you experienced this sensation in the past, was the feeling considered to be an expression of your Other Body? If not, under what label, concept or interpretation was it placed? Too often, our natural senses are thwarted by cultural wanglers. We "toilet train" these senses to bond or addict us to society's Toxic Triad ways. Can you remember any incidents, beliefs or people who removed you from enjoying this particular natural sense? Are these wranglers (wronglers) alive in you? If you saw somebody enjoying this natural sense, what might come to mind?

Match yourself with a person you know. What attractions to them do you recognize in yourself? Recognize that if you sense them, they are also some part of you.

* *̊ *

Resonate: Once you have gone to an attractive natural area and thankfully gained its consent to do and Validate your natural attraction, this activity helps you further register the natural attraction through many of your different senses. For example, connect to your validated attraction through your sense of Music: Experimentally hum or sing a few musical notes until you find one which you feel resonates with (best represents or registers) your validated attraction. Once you make this connection, you have learned to know the attraction more fully by resonating with it through your sense of Music. Now hum a note that represents how you feel and then find another natural attraction that fits that note.

Resonate with an attraction through your sense of Distance. Move towards it or away from it to discover at what point it feels most attractive and supportive. Further each different attraction that calls you by discovering its intensities: softest-loudest, brightest-dullest, largest-smallest.

Repeat the above resonating experience by selecting other senses by which you want to sense this attraction. Through them, you can more fully resonate with it at will and thereby strengthen it. For example: You can be attracted to the sound of a flowing stream and attempt to resonate with that sound through the senses of community, taste, trust, smell, compassion, belonging, etc.

Repeat the resonating experience using your attractions to a person you like and a person you don't think you like.

Each time we resonate with a natural attraction through a different sense, we get to know the attraction and ourselves in a new, more fulfilling and holistic way. This holds true for the natural attractions we sense in people as well as in places. For example, if you are not resonating with a person with respect to their loudness, try sensing them musically.

A methodical way to better know yourself and nature is to go through the list of senses in Appendix B here or pages RWN 48-50 one at a time. For each sense, locate a natural attraction, and then resonate with that attraction through each of the other 52 listed senses. Do this as long as it feels attractive to do it, then stop and continue it at some other time.

Past Participant's reactions: The rock glowed a little brighter every time I got to know it through a different sense. This is like a combination of all the activities I've learned to date. It feels like I think Us must feel and know itself. Definitely a way to increase my spirituality and contact with Higher Power. I found it hard to do this, but each time I accomplished it, I really enjoyed the results.

* * *

Appreciate: Once you have gone to an attractive natural area and thankfully gained its consent to do and Validate your natural attraction,. By calling to you and touching you, this natural attraction has given you good feelings. This activity benefits you with the value of conscientiously thanking it for having given your life attractive enjoyable sensations. This activity intensifies that value.

Raise the stakes for how you express your thankfulness. Honor this entity with a physical act, gift, or spoken words. Honor it for sharing its attractiveness with you as well as for sustaining the flow of the global life community through you. Honor it for fulfilling your natural wants so that you don't excessively want. How else might you thank it without hurting it? Value Collision: If you are thanking a tree and the gift you give it is to urinate on its root area, does it appreciate the gift? All of nature contains mutual attractions. If you appreciate this natural attraction, it appreciates you and expresses it. What gift does this area give you? Can you take a physical gift from it to help you remember it? Write why you deserve to have this

VALUE INDEX My degree of attraction to the information on this page:

1	2	3	4	5	6	7	8	9	10
None				Moderate			Strong		

IF IMPORTANT, WHY?

gift. Repeat this activity by enjoying an attraction you have to another person and similarly expressing appreciation for it.

* * *

Trust: Once you have gone to an attractive natural area and thankfully gained its consent to do and Validate your natural attraction increase, how much you trust thinking with your Other Body?. With its consent, see how close you can to get to that same attraction in another natural are area. What wrangler stories, if any, stop you from getting closer. What prevents you from trusting the love of your Other Body that you discover through these activities?

Think about

>How much do you trust the existence and powers of NNIAAL,
>The material and the nonmaterial world of nature being your "subconscious mind,"
>The natural world consisting entirely of NNIAAL.
>Our society being at war with nature.
>Your Other Body, Nature, NNIAAL and your "inner child" being identical.
>Try to identify where you feel reconnecting with nature is not trustable.

Write a short statement explaining why you might want to trust and continue to use this process or parts of it. Each time you find your trust is weaker than you would like it to be, with the consent of that area, bring a friend to that place and teach him or her to do some of these activities that most attract you. Does your trust and comfort increase?

You may sensibly demand of your Toxic Triad that your reasoning and language senses learn to trust the attractions, senses and feelings that you obtain from your nature experiences. It is reasonable for you to expect the Triad to trust them because your natural sensations and feelings, including those in the Triad, are facts of life. They are as real as sunshine, water, air and soil because they are part of them. Use the activities to give you experiences that support and strengthen your trust.

* * *

Celebrate: Once you have gone to an attractive natural area and thankfully gained its consent to do and Validate your natural attraction, To help your Toxic Triad consciousness integrate your Other Body nature connections, in a notebook write a Haiku verse or short poem which expresses your thoughts and feelings about connecting with this attraction. (A Haiku is three line prose whose first line contains 5 syllables, second line contains 7 syllables and third closing line contains 5 syllables.) It helps language connect with and strengthen your senses and vice versa. For example, for connecting with orange autumn leaves you might write:

Orange sunrise leaves,

Awaken deep within me,

The dawn of being.

Upon completing the Haiku, alone or with a friend, assume a posture and/or dance motion which you feel states your good feelings with regard to a Toxic Triad to an Other Body inclusive experience. Hold your position/motions for at least 30 seconds. If necessary, defend yourself from criticism coming from within or around you. Repeat this activity with an attraction you find in a person, including yourself. Your habitual closeted thinking may demean you for participating in this celebration. An internal wrangler may label you as "touchy-feely" "childish" "unscientific" "fuzzy thinking" "far out" or "spiritual." Declare your independence. Protect your pursuit of happiness, your good feeling connections with your Other Body, if you want them to flourish, satisfy and fulfill you. Nobody else can do this for you. Do your dance, more energetically express your Other Body truth. Share your Haikus. They enable language to connect people with Nature. Use them in to letters to friends. Decorate, frame and display them. They are the reason why God invented refrigerator doors.

"Truth is by nature self-evident. As soon as you remove the cobwebs of ignorance that surround it, it shines clear."- **Mahatma Gandhi circa 1935**

"When the facts change, I change my mind. What do you do, sir?" - **John Maynard Keynes circa 1936**

"All children are born geniuses. 9,999 out of every 10,000 are swiftly, inadvertently, degeniused by grown ups."- **Buckminster Fuller circa 1960**

VALUE INDEX My degree of attraction to the information on this page:

1	2	3	4	5	6	7	8	9	10
None				Moderate			Strong		

IF IMPORTANT, WHY?

APPENDIX C

THE ANATOMY OF INSTITUTIONS

"When I arrived at my assigned camping place it was wild, as if nobody had ever been there. I figured out a way to get through the brush to the outhouse, about 70 yards away and I came back a different way. The next day, I remembered the way there and also returned the same way since it was easier to find now that I had tramped it down a bit. I repeated this for about two weeks and when my friends began to arrive at the campsite I showed them the outhouse trail and they used it. You could tell who the new arrivals were from folks who had been there awhile because the latter knew the trail and would instruct the newcomers. Then Mark found an easier trail and some of the group used it, but mostly the newcomers. The earlier folks were accustomed to the old trail and stayed with it as a habit, even placing a sign on it saying "Outhouse Trail." It had become ingrained on the landscape, in memory and now in written language, almost an institution or sub-culture for "Olders" because the newcomers continued using Mark's trail."

For the Olders, their senses had been directed and rewarded by using the old trail. They found the Outhouse and they also survived another day, so why change? Survival is a powerful yet overlooked reward until of course, it is threatened. Then we fight for it. As part of our Other Body (Planet Earth) survival sensibility the senses of Direction, Exploration, Place, Community, Trust, Reason, Language, Distance, Motion and others had bonded/fixated to the old trail. If the trail had been found to be toxic, those who insisted on continuing to use it would have been identified as being addicted or socialized (brainwashed) to it through past repetition and rewards.

The old trail had changed from being a discovery experience to an authority of its own, an Institution rather than an exploration or a choice. This was true, too, of much of the original wildness of the original campsite. It was replaced by social and technological structures regarding the table, fire pit, tent sites, clotheslines, camping equipment, garbage storage, their placement and rules for using them. I became stressed as I recognized that artifacts and rules had replaced some of the excitement, discovery and wilderness values for me. The sound of talking, of stories from and about elsewhere, replaced bird songs, hanging laundry replaced the wonderful view. These were all sense grabbers in that I was unaware that my Other Body had been captured and become accustomed to them. I thought it was progress until I noticed how stressed I was. It was exactly what happened to each of us in early childhood as our Other Body was "socialized" into adulthood. I could imagine if it continued the campsite could become the nature-disconnected stories, discontents and impact of "civilization" and our bonded dependency on the questionable ways of its institutions.

Like a robust religion or corporation, the army is a good example of how a strong institution works. Its inroads, trespasses and sensory rewards are found, more or less, in every institution. Keep a look out for them if you don't want them to secretly control your life in a destructive way. They are dedicated to make you into a cultural object that dances to the isolated will of fame, greed, progress and economics that capture and injure our Other Body. You lose your last name as it changes from "Jones" to Consumer or Member.

- The Dogma of the army ties our Triad of the senses of Language, Reason and Consciousness to the army's stated purpose, its story, real or imaginary and its role in our culture

- Army Commandments, Rules and Regulations focus our natural senses of Reason Fear and Pain into behaviors that fulfill the dogma

- The Hierarchy of the army, it officers and rule enforcers, actively restrict and direct senses of Nurturing, Language, Community, Pain, Motion and Reason to respond to army dogma.

- The Credo encapsulates the Dogma to capture the senses of Literacy and Consciousness

- The Uniform captures our natural sense of Self, Camouflage, Color and Design; we are what we wear.

- Army Rituals habituate most of our natural senses to army dogma, via repetition and rules.

- Army Terminology holds the natural senses of Language and Consciousness to terms exclusive to the army, not to society at large.
- Army Schedule captures our Other Body sense of "Now" Time and directs what we

will do when.

• The Paraphernalia of the army ties most natural senses to materials that fulfill the dogma

• Martial Music attaches our senses of Music and Rhythm to respond to army spirit and dogma.

• Army Colors and Logos attach our senses of Sight, Design and Color to army insignias and hierarchy

• Army Heros attach our sense of self and community to individuals who have gone beyond the ordinary as enactors of the dogma.

• Army Economics attract our money (survival) to support Army Dogma.

• Army Doctrine and Dominion culturally influences our senses to its Dogma during early childhood as well as makes political inroads often in conjunction with army economics and propaganda.

• The army Value Symbol, the flag, captures many natural senses and their spirit so that, when stressed or commanded, our Other Body automatically depends upon and responds to the army as a story or institution. We almost worship the Value Symbol as a logo; we often wear it, defend it and may go as far as die for it.

Some institutions don't have all these characteristics or their full intensity, but all institutions have some of them. The institution of formal Education is one that prepares us to accept and join the others as human objects whose Toxic Triad is psychologically enslaved to them.

Too often we don't choose to join institutions; rather we're born into them. Try and change yourself or anybody else that's in one if you want to see how intensely an institution affects a person. This even takes place in recovery groups when Nature as higher power is criticized as a replacement of God or Jesus, even though the guidelines say you have a choice. Nature is wonderful in that, being non-literate, it has no dogma other than its attraction to seek and build natural attraction relationships

VALUE INDEX My degree of attraction to the information on this page:

1	2	3	4	5	6	7	8	9	10
	None				Moderate			Strong	

IF IMPORTANT, WHY?

The Value Symbol of an institution is the most frightening thing of all because it gives directions to many of our institution-connected senses without us knowing it. People wear value symbols as decorations, their style as well as hidden dictators who seek your money and not necessarily your well-being.

August 6, 2007: Researchers gave a group of 3-5 year old children two identical servings of many different kinds of food. The only difference between the two servings was that one was wrapped in a McDonald's wrapper, the other in a plain wrapper.

Overwhelmingly, the children said the identical food placed in the McDonalds' wrapper tasted better. Their psyche had been misled and corrupted. At this early age, their natural senses and sensibilities had already been prejudicially socialized by the money-making Value Symbol, story and images conveyed on the McDonalds' wrapper. That story, along with its questionable values and effects, had distorted and stressed the children's natural ability to think and feel appropriately with respect to their natural sense of Taste. Their healthy natural attachment to healthy food had been polluted and disturbed. They were partly delusional. They had been robbed of part of their vital natural intelligence and its joy. One of their attachments to the life of their Other Body had been "McBurgered."

Now, ask yourself these critical questions:

Where are the institutions that re-connect our Zombiness, -our Toxic Triad senses of Reason, Consciousness and Literacy- back to our Other Body in a good way to help us reverse our disorders?

Who is helping our Other Body teach us to be Earth Avatars as part of our recovery from Industrial Society's undeclared war to conquer our Other Body?

Has the thinking of some people been institutionalized so that they feel they must hassle folks who know nature is their higher power and who have been given the right to turn to nature's powers in the 12-step program?

APPENDIX D

AN ACTIVITY FOR PROBLEMS OR QUESTIONS

When problems arise, such as being ridiculed for recognizing that we learn to war against the essence of our Other Body (NNIAAL), or that we don't register our Other Body via at least 54 natural sensations, you can use this activity to help deal with them:

Our Other Body as our Teacher:

1. Think about a real problem or question that you have about some aspect of life or of your life. If no question arises, use the generic question: "What would you like to teach me?"

2. Thankfully gain permission from an attractive natural area to visit it and help you do this activity.

3. Using the same permission process, ask attractions in this area, one after the other if necessary, if they will consent to be your teacher. When one consents, thank it for befriending you.

4. With your eyes closed and then open, sense as many attractions as you can that are part of this attraction, For example, the color, motion , temperature, form, texture etc. of a rock, (or tree, pond, etc.).

5. Make ample physical contact with the rock. Touch it with your hands and feet if possible, Keep your eyes on it.

6. Sense the essence of the rock, What one sensation resonates as being it?

7. Give that essence a name such as: Rock Mortal, Rockness, Rock Being, Rocking, My Rock Body or Now.

8. Ask this essence, by name, the question you have. If you have no question, ask it what it would like to teach you i.e. "Rock Body, what would you like to teach me?"

9. Wait for a response to appear in words or images. Validate. Say the response aloud.

Write it down. Thank the essence for sharing this response with you.

10. Now imagine stepping into the essence of this natural attraction and becoming it. You are Rockness.

11. As this essence, picture yourself as you were when you asked it the question in 6. Tell that image of yourself the answer you gave it in 9. Then tell that same response to yourself as you know your self at this moment.

12. As this essence, thank your human self for honoring you by seeking you and trusting you to respond to the question.

13. Return to being yourself here and now.

14. Thank this attraction for being, for participating in your life and for teaching you.

15. Write the response of the essence down and read it after sleeping on it for one night, and then again 10 hours later.

16. If you want additional knowledge about the response you received, with it in mind, do the SEVMRATC series, or parts of it that are attractive at that time. Then repeat this activity.

17. Repeat this activity with the attractive inner nature of person who you feel could teach you something you want to know.

APPENDIX E

THE 54 NATURAL SENSES

"My lifelong communion with trees allows me to know them without sight or language. The beautiful elucidation of fifty-four senses, below, has given me gorgeous language with which to tell this story, one I have struggled to share my whole life. I don't want to ever sound mysterious, or other worldly. For me this communication has just been a fact of life. But how to explain it to others? I still feel there is an element of my understanding that is nameless, and so loving it needs no words. But to have a natural sense, a new brain language to describe this experience in a way others can understand, is lovely, just lovely."

YOUR NATURAL SYSTEMS LEGACY: Identify and benefit from fifty-four natural attraction senses (Webstrings) you have learned to forget to remember.

From Reconnecting With Nature and Educating, Counseling and Healing With Nature by Michael J. Cohen, Ph.D.

Between the years of 1961-1978, researcher Guy Murchie made an exhaustive inquiry. He painstakingly scrutinized scientific studies about natural senses, studies that appeared in many hundreds of books and periodicals during those 17 years.

In 1986 Murchie told me that scientific methodology and research had identified over eighty different biological senses/sensitivities that pervade the natural world. He said he additionally verified this through authorities at the Harvard Biological Laboratories. All these senses, he said, he clumped together as 31 senses for literary convenience in his book The Seven Mysteries of Life published by Houghton Mifflin in 1978.

Murchie's dedicated efforts deserve our applause, thanks and confidence.

From Murchie's original collection, I identified 54 natural senses that my students and I had experienced during my 26 years living and teaching outdoors. I have listed them below. Each

VALUE INDEX My degree of attraction to the information on this page:

1	2	3	4	5	6	7	8	9	10
	None			Moderate			Strong		

IF IMPORTANT, WHY?

is an inherent natural attraction string in the web of life, a genetically rooted web-of-life strand (webstring) that helps to hold the world together, including people, through universal natural attraction communications, guidance and motivations. The 54th sense, "natural attraction" has recently been added since the discovery of the Higgs Boson.

There are, of course, many additional natural sensitivities found in nature that humans do not naturally need to register for survival, ultra violet light and high frequency sounds being prime examples.

Most misunderstood are the naturally attractive contributions of the discomforting senses like pain, distress and fear. We often forget that we might seriously burn our hand on a hot stove if pain did not signal and motivate us to immediately find some other attractive place to place our hand. Each of these senses (25-27) serves as an attractive and welcome motivating signal from nature to find additional webstring attractions to support our lives (See Chapter 13 in Reconnecting With Nature).

Although Ames, Gesell, Pearce, Rivlin, Gravelle, Samuels, Sheppard, Sheldrake, Spelke, LePoncin, Wynn and many scores of other researchers have, since Murchie, further validated our multisensory nature, the full significance of it has yet to be recognized by contemporary society. Our prejudicial addiction to our nature-separated lives and thinking keeps webstring natural attraction senses and their value hidden from our immediate awareness. For this reason they and we are frustrated with un-fulfillment, frystratuions and very challenging problems.

Our economy fuels itself by keeping our webstrings discontent, further irritating them through advertising and then selling us products that satisfy our irritation. However, when unadulterated, our natural attraction webstring senses are an essence of nature in action. Each of them attracts our consciousness to the whole of the natural webstring world and its self-correcting ways, and this includes the natural systems in ourselves and other people. Each is an intelligence that helps us feel Planet Earth as our other body and mother.

As our good experiences in natural areas demonstrate, our natural senses when connected to nature produce fulfillments, sensory satisfactions that reduce stress and its related disorders. In addition, the connection's "side effects" increase social and environmental well-being rather than deteriorating it. Any individual who invented a pill that produced these results would be a billionaire. However, the pill can't be created as there is no known substitute for Nature's

Dance of the eons, in and around us.

Whenever our society encourages our new brain to conquer nature and the natural, we learn to conquer and subdue our natural senses and their expression of our genetic makeup. Our 5-leg, abstracting, nature disconnected sense of reason, exalts the few senses that our stories use to take over our other natural senses and the natural world. We exploit and demean the remaining 45 natural senses that their 4-leg, sensing/feeling ways tell us about how the natural world works its perfection and enable us to participate in the process.

Overwhelmed and numbed, our webstring senses are a vast missing part of a responsible story about Earth, ourselves, community and about how and when to act where. Without webstrings registering in consciousness we are "half vast." As Carl Jung and others have noted, our abstract thinking is no more reasonable or discriminating, logical and consistent than are our feelings.

Nature has taught me that our abstract 5-leg thinking in conjunction with conscious sensory 4-leg contact with attractions in natural areas can be the 9-leg way we learn to put our natural senses into culturally reasonable words. Our challenge is recognize that the excessively nature separated parts of ourselves and our culture are unreasonable.

We desperately need to think with nature's wise ability to maintain and restore life, without producing our problems. That wisdom prevents and stops our society's destructive actions against ourselves others and the environment.

The absence of more than 45 webstrings from our conscious thinking is the mother of our collective madness, of our runaway wars, pollution, dysfunction, disease, mental illness,apathy, abusiveness and violence. Without experiencing these webstrings, our consciousness abandons our natural sensory "inner child," and the inner child in other people and species. It disintegrates the creative passions that normally bring about community, balance and positive change peacefully.

Anybody can choose to help reverse this destructive situation by choosing to learn and teach

VALUE INDEX My degree of attraction to the information on this page:

1	2	3	4	5	6	7	8	9	10
	None				Moderate			Strong	

IF IMPORTANT, WHY?

how, via the Web of Life Imperative, to reconnect with webstrings and nature.

I offer the following list of 54 natural senses with this important reminder: Each sense is a distinct 4-leg webstring attraction that in nature has no name for itself, for nature does not use names. Each webstring can awaken many natural parts of us when we use it to connect with the natural world in the environment and people. That touchy-feely, hands-on, connecting experience, not this list of senses, catalyzes personal wisdom, growth and balance. This list only provides information in 5-leg language. It brings it on our screen of consciousness and feeds and guides our senses of reason and language, our story way of knowing. However, without passion (apathy), 5-leg reason and language are ineffective when it comes to disengaging our destructive bonds and enjoying responsible behavior, growth and change. For example, even though cigarette labels and research show cigarettes to be harmful, many people continue to smoke them. Reason and language and consciousness are only 6% of our inherent means to know and love nature, life and each other. Our 51 other 4-leg sense groups complete the process. Without them awake and well in our consciousness, we experience apathy and hurt, we don't participate and our problems continue.

Nature centered 9-leg thinking uses the list of senses, below, in conjunction with visiting natural areas and with exposing our indoor conditioning to the many natural senses in us that we may awaken in nature. To do this is reasonable, for after we experience a natural sensory attraction, knowing and speaking its right name places that sensation in our new brain consciousness. There we can think with it and be motivated by it. This process non-verbally connects, rejuvenates and educates us. It extends us to safely reach into the natural world in order to more fully sense and make sense of our lives and all of life. It works because once we experience the perfection of nature's restorative process and wisdom, we own it. We never fully return to our former way of knowing.

THE FIFTY FOUR NATURAL WEBSTRING SENSES AND SENSITIVITIES

The Radiation Senses
1. Sense of light and sight, including polarized light.
2. Sense of seeing without eyes such as heliotropism or the sun sense of plants.
3. Sense of color.
4. Sense of moods and identities attached to colors.
5. Sense of awareness of one's own visibility or invisibility and consequent camouflaging.
6. Sensitivity to radiation other than visible light including radio waves, X rays, etc.

7. Sense of Temperature and temperature change.

8. Sense of season including ability to insulate, hibernate and winter sleep.

9. Electromagnetic sense and polarity which includes the ability to generate current (as in the nervous system and brain waves) or other energies.

The Feeling Senses

10. Hearing including resonance, vibrations, sonar and ultrasonic frequencies.

11. Awareness of pressure, particularly underground, underwater, and to wind and air.

12. Sensitivity to gravity.

13. The sense of excretion for waste elimination and protection from enemies.

14. Feel, particularly touch on the skin.

15. Sense of weight, gravity and balance.

16. Space or proximity sense.

17. Coriolus sense or awareness of effects of the rotation of the Earth.

18. Sense of motion. Body movement sensations and sense of mobility.

The Chemical Senses

19. Smell with and beyond the nose.

20. Taste with and beyond the tongue.

21. Appetite or hunger for food, water and air.

22. Hunting, killing or food obtaining urges.

23. Humidity sense including thirst, evaporation control and the acumen to find water or evade a flood.

24. Hormonal sense, as to pheromones and other chemical stimuli.

The Mental Senses.

(25-27 are attractions to seek additional natural attractions in order to support and strengthen well-being).

25. Pain, external and internal.

26. Mental or spiritual distress.

27. Sense of fear, dread of injury, death or attack

28. Procreative urges including sex awareness, courting, love, mating, paternity and raising young.

29. Sense of play, sport, humor, pleasure and laughter.

30. Sense of physical place, navigation senses including detailed awareness of land and seascapes, of the positions of the sun, moon and stars.

VALUE INDEX My degree of attraction to the information on this page:

1   2   3   4   5   6   7   8   9   10

None   Moderate   Strong

IF IMPORTANT, WHY?

31. Sense of time and rhythm.

32. Sense of electromagnetic fields.

33. Sense of weather changes.

34. Sense of emotional place, of community, belonging, support, trust and thankfulness.

35. Sense of self including friendship, companionship, and power.

36. Domineering and territorial sense.

37. Colonizing sense including compassion and receptive awareness of one's fellow creatures, sometimes to the degree of being absorbed into a superorganism.

38. Horticultural sense and the ability to cultivate crops, as is done by ants that grow fungus, by fungus who farm algae, or birds that leave food to attract their prey.

39. Language and articulation sense, used to express feelings and convey information in every medium from the bees' dance to human literature.

40. Sense of humility, appreciation, ethics.

41. Senses of form and design.

42. Sense of reason, including memory and the capacity for logic and science.

43. Sense of mind and consciousness.

44. Intuition or subconscious deduction.

45. Aesthetic sense, including creativity and appreciation of beauty, music, literature, form, design and drama.

46. Psychic capacity such as foreknowledge, clairvoyance, clairaudience, psychokinesis, astral projection and possibly certain animal instincts and plant sensitivities.

47. Sense of biological and astral time, awareness of past, present and future events.

48. The capacity to hypnotize other creatures.

49. Relaxation and sleep including dreaming, meditation, brain wave awareness.

50. Sense of pupation including cocoon building and metamorphosis.

51. Sense of excessive stress and capitulation.

52. Sense of survival by joining a more established organism.

53. Spiritual sense, including conscience, capacity for sublime love, ecstasy, a sense of sin, profound sorrow and sacrifice

54. Sense of unity, of natural attraction as the singular mother essence and source of all our other senses.

This list explains how, sense by sense, nature 9-leg connects with itself in us, through us and to people and places around us. It suggests that we can consciously engage in this process. It validates Dr. David Viscott's proposal that feelings are the truth, that we don't live in the real world when we ignore what we are feeling. Our nature-separated lives disengage and de-energize these senses. Applying the organic psychology of the Natural Systems Thinking Process allows nature, the mother of these senses and feelings, to nurture and strengthen them, to rejuvenate them to normal. The process gives them enough energy to appear on our nature desensitized screen of consciousness and green our thinking.

THE SENSES AT HOME IN NATURE

"The experience I'm recalling is a trip I took with a friend to Mt Lemmon in Tucson. After a half mile hike back into the forest at the 9,000 foot in elevation level we found a mammoth rock. It was the size of a house and half buried in the earth. We both laid on our brother rock for about 20 minutes. It was a cool sunny (cloud) day and we were surrounded by a forest of massively beautiful pine trees. The rock was oh so warm and comforting to embrace as the sun shone on my body. The contrast of the warm rock and the cool breeze was so wonderful. Wind softly blowing in my ears. The ultimate reward was loosing all my stress and anxiety from my entire body. A physical therapist would have charged me $150 to do what nature did for zip. My senses registered colors, sounds, feelings, aromas, sensations, moods, contracts, textures, sizes, distance. I stopped controlling the world and let mother earth breath for me. I felt the texture of the rock and the sensation of holding up the world on my back. It was weightless and comforting to support. The sounds of the nearby creek and the many bustling creatures were a symphony of natures' voices all welcoming me to stay as long as wanted. The smell of pine was in the air. All senses were on maximum open channel and I melted into moment with ease. It was only my natural sensory attraction connections to the natural area that provided these rewards. I have never, in all my years of public or higher education been taught anything about what I just experienced."

AN ACTIVITY FOR SENSING THE SENSES

"With 20 years experience with outdoor education and adventure based learning, I have facilitated "willow in the wind" activities many times. A person stands stiff in the center of a circle of people, close their eyes and leans over as if to fall down. The people in the circle prop up the middle person to prevent falling and state the name of the natural sense they represent that is supporting the person. Unfortunately, I could not form a group at this time so I decided to improvise as follows:

There is a long circular trail that runs through thickly forested high ground overlooking the Chattahoochee River. I used this trail to replace the circle of humans called for in the classic

VALUE INDEX My degree of attraction to the information on this page:

1   2   3   4   5   6   7   8   9   10
     None   Moderate   Strong
IF IMPORTANT, WHY?

"willow in the wind" activity, and used natural attractions as the "pushers" and my sensory responses as the "catchers". I respectfully sought permission to do the activity and began walking along a narrow dirt and gravel road toward the trail head a short distance away. As I walked along the road, slowly cleansing my lens of perception by turning my attention from things artificial to the vast natural area surrounding me, something in my peripheral vision compelled me to stop and look. I saw a large, beautifully formed, yellow and brown acorn, and as I continued to scan the ground, I saw many more. Senses that responded: sense of color; sense of moods and identities attached to colors; sense of season; senses of form and design. Reaching the trail head, I turned off the road and continued my slow walk with senses now more attuned to the purpose. I had not gone far when once again my peripheral vision alerted me to stop and connect with a small bush growing along side the trail. A single, dime-sized, brilliant red fruit attached to the bush stood out from the muted colors of its background. The fruit's red, thick skin stood open and appeared as a five-petal flower with a shiny red seed attached to the base of each petal. Senses that responded: sense of color; sense of season; sense of moods and identities attached to colors; sense of season; senses of form and design; sense of emotional place, of community, belonging, support, trust and thankfulness; aesthetic sense; sense of humility, appreciation, ethics; sense of self. Continuing on the trail, I came to a huge, recently fallen, oak tree that lay across the trail and blocked it. Always interested in such scenes, I stopped and started my analysis of the visible evidence when suddenly a close by and unexpected sound of rustling leaves startled me. Looking around for the source, I saw nothing, and turned my attention back to the tree only to be startled again by the same sound followed by another and another. Finally, I had the answer: large acorns sporadically dropping from tall oak trees crashed into the thick layer of dry leaves that covered the ground surrounding me. Senses that responded: sense of hearing; sense of fear; sense of physical place; sense of humor. From this point, the trailed climbed steeply to the high ridge top and a view of the river flowing swiftly far below. As I slowly made my way up the steep trail, I realized the activation of yet another sense. Sense that responded: sense of weight, gravity and balance. After reaching the top, I paused to spend a few minutes admiring the view, but before I could focus on the river, a slight motion on the ground near my feet grabbed my attention. I stared down at the tiniest snake I have ever seen. Because of its small size, it took awhile to identify it as a snake. Its amazingly tiny forked tongue and lack of legs finally convinced me. Keenly interested in this fellow being, I admired its beautiful color: dark blue with a thin bright yellow line encircling the body just behind the head. Senses that responded: Sense of light and sight; sense of color; sense of moods and identities attached to color; sense of emotional place, of community, belonging, support, trust and thankfulness; senses of form and design. As I looked down at the ancient river below, these same senses remained engaged. From this point, I continued on the trail back toward the road near my starting point.

I discovered that properly functioning senses are essential for a meaningful and appropriately balanced life and require maintenance through frequent and experiential interaction with the natural world.

The characteristics of western culture tend to diminish and distort the proper functioning of natural senses, which in turn distorts the accuracy of perception.

My experience with nature shows me that I am a person who gets good feelings from being outdoors in a natural area and who enjoys exercising my senses by interacting and connecting with natural objects in a natural area. I get pleasure from seeing a tiny snake using its tiny tongue to sense the area around it. I would be deeply distressed to lose my ability to experience being in tune with nature."

VALUE INDEX My degree of attraction to the information on this page:

1	2	3	4	5	6	7	8	9	10
None				Moderate			Strong		

IF IMPORTANT, WHY?

APPENDIX F

New Vistas Dawn: The Only Life of its Kind that we Know

Michael J. Cohen, How Nature Works (1986)

NOTE: The experience described below occurred 13 years after, in 1952, I began exploring why people were friendlier and relaxed while they were in a natural area. During this period I lived with others for extended periods in natural settings in Mother Earth and I developed ways of interpreting nature that helped demonstrate that, "Nature knows what it is doing and what to do to maintain its perfection as a paradise. Because we are part of nature, people in natural settings have the ability to sense and embrace nature's ways and this improves their relationships with themselves and each other."

> "The senses were, in Eden, spread over the whole being. It might seem, then, that our bodies still live in Eden, but our minds refuse to know it."
> - **William Blake circa 1790**

Deep in the bowels of Grand Canyon National Park, a spectacle of color and towering cliffs marks the place where Bright Angel Creek joins the Colorado River. There, in 1966, a thunderstorm on a broiling August day cracked my twentieth-century prejudices about life and the land.

To keep cool in this desert country, I hiked shirtless. Occasionally, I munched potato chips to maintain my body's salt level. As I did when I originally passed Phantom Canyon, when I crossed the bridge spanning the muddy Colorado my hand again touched my surprisingly icy stomach while the air temperature was 120 degrees. My years of scientific training went to work: "This is a cooling mechanism. Evaporating sweat molecules carry away excess body heat, leaving this residue of salt on my skin." It never occurred to me that miracles, not just molecules, kept my body temperate while the sun scorched the world about me.

Thunderclouds moved in from the southwest. "Now you're going to see something amazing," I told the twenty expedition members who accompanied me. "As the thunderstorm rains,

VALUE INDEX My degree of attraction to the information on this page:

1	2	3	4	5	6	7	8	9	10
None				Moderate				Strong	

IF IMPORTANT, WHY?

the heat evaporates the raindrops. We'll see the rain fall, but we won't get wet down here." We were a mile below the rim.

I knew this would happen. It had happened almost every year on this outdoor learning trek, which I inaugurated in 1959. The expedition students looked skeptical, but the prospect of a "dry" storm excited them.

The dark clouds rolled in and poured torrents, drenching us while we stood agape. "Hey, look everybody, I'm really dry," taunted one soaked girl, while smirking group members scurried for cover, gleefully mumbling, "Oh sure, Mike, it never rains in the Grand Canyon."

How often those words would assail me that summer and in the years to come. Somehow, most students I worked with heard about the incident. Whenever I came close to predicting anything I'd hear "Sure Mike, and it never rains in the Grand Canyon."

But the skies opened up and rain it did. Quickly the canyon cooled. Like soap suds rinsed from shampooed hair, the red sands and clays of the Grand Canyon sloshed over the thousand-foot inner gorge walls that loomed above us. Everywhere, blood-red water cascaded and the roaring river turned from tan to murky maroon. The trembling canyon felt like a vein gathering and carrying blood. For a moment, I sensed we were in a gigantic organism's bloodstream. The flowing landscape seemed alive. And just like my evaporating sweat had cooled me, evaporating rain now cooled the canyon, furthering this sense of aliveness.

As I watched Grand Canyon salts run downriver to the sea, I wondered, "Why does the sea never become too salty, or the land never too hot for life? This is part of the intelligence of life, it is aware of what it's doing." Then it all came together as the self-balancing homeostasis of life that Walter Cannon described in Wisdom of the Body.

I put words to what I was feeling. I experienced Planet Earth as a living organism that knows how to survive. I was dumbfounded. I tried to dismiss the idea but it hung on as if for dear life. I thought I was the only person in the world who had ever entertained this notion and I spent time considering whether I should embrace it and risk credibility or support. I'd be seen as a freak. I would be walking an unnecessary giant step into the beyond. Crazier still, I felt I could take this risk because the earth would back me up like a loving mother or family. That was nuts. Just thirty minutes earlier planet Earth, to me, was a dead geologic structure floating around the sun.

I moved onto a crack in the ancient cliff face and it felt like the warm rocks smiled at me. Slowly, I made the decision. I'd live with the idea that Earth acted like, or could be, a living organism. I immediately felt like part of me had walked into a different world and married it. It still does.

I recognized myself and the planet as living kin, There was nothing I could find that it did not do that I did not do, except that I could talk, I was literate, however we were both alive.

To survive, the wilderness and I share the challenge of becoming too hot, cold, salty or toxic. The living planet's biology, geology and chemistry are its metabolism; night-day, night-day, night-day its heartbeat. Warm evaporating inland seas serve as kidneys; air and water are flowing plasma. In congress, all aspects of Earth compose a planet-sized intelligence, a wise gigantic self-regulating plant cell whose life approaches perfection. The cell knows how to organize, preserve and regenerate itself, and how to create and sustain its diverse life without pollution, war insanity or loneliness. Perhaps Earth is a fertilized egg of the universe. It is the only life of its kind that we know. As such, it deserves protection under the endangered species act.

Self-doubt possessed me. It was 1965, sixteen years before I heard of the Gaia Hypothesis, three years before James Lovelock even conceived it. My understanding of Gaia grew as I learned that every eighty million years the salt content of the sea doubles, but the sea never becomes more saline; Mars and Venus, the two planets surrounding Earth, become warmer as the sun gets hotter, but Earth's temperature stays within the limits necessary for life's existence, and our atmosphere maintains oxygen in amounts neither too great nor too small for all life to survive.

Scientific investigations continue to validate what I sensed that day in the Grand Canyon. They show that life will succumb to pollution, chemical and physical forces. To survive, it needs the grace and self-correcting, purifying powers that help it balance restore and recycle itself.

Recent findings indicate that Planet Earth's biology, physiology and geology are tightly linked into a single indivisible attraction process that resonates within and about us and can reasonably register in our thinking through the science of Natural Attraction Ecology. "Organism Earth" not only shows signs of life but, in addition, it registers itself in our natural mind, senses and feelings. For example, its water cycle includes us due to our natural senses of thirst and excretion. This possibility has become more accepted in our society and has helped others enjoy experiences similar to mine.

In 1985 a National Audubon Society Intenational Symposium was convened based on my observations that Earth was a living organism. In 2010 The People's Conference on Climate Change defined the rights that our planet should have as a living being. Contemporary thinking has yet to recognize that Natural Attraction Ecology gives us the presently missing/ omitted process that helps us implement giving Mother Earth these rights and relating accordingly.

In the year 2010, James Cameron's film depiction of the planet Pandora and the relationship of the Na'vi to it are the closest image I've seen to what I discovered in the Grand Canyon with respect to the truth of humanity and Mother Earth that I convey in my Webstring Model, books and courses

What Cameron represents in the fantasy of his film, I have demonstrated to be true and accessible to anybody, now, on Earth, via my scientific process of Educating, Counseling and Healing With Nature (ECHN). My books and courses enable an individual's thoughts and feelings to choose to make this therapeutic connection with authentic nature as an organism or living cathedral.

APPENDIX G

REFERENCES: Topics and Further Information

1. MODEL OF PROJECT NATURECONNECT Cohen, M. J. 2008, Educating Counseling and Healing With Nature Illumina Publishing.
http://www.ecopsych.com/ksanity.html

2. OLD BRAIN/NEW BRAIN Cohen, M. J. 1995, Education and Counseling With Nature: A Greening of Psychotherapy. The Interspych Newsletter, Vol 2, Issue 4
http://www.ecopsych.com/counseling.html

3. LEARNED FROM EXPERIENCE Project NatureConnect: The Miracle of Something from Nothing
http://www.ecopsych.com/journalessence.html

4. ATTRACTION AS SCIENCE Project NatureConnect 2007, Natural Attraction Ecology
http://www.naturalattractionecology.com

5. OUTCOMES Project NatureConnect, 1996, A Survey of Participants
http://www.ecopsych.com/survey.html

6. 54 NATURAL SENSES Project NatureConnect, 1990, Connecting With Nature, World Peace University Press
http://www.ecopsych.com/insight53senses.html

7. EARTH AS A LIVING ORGANISM Project NatureConnect, 1986 New Vistas Dawn: The Only Life of its Kind That We Know, "Reconnecting With Nature", Ecopress 1997
http://www.ecopsych.com/livingplanetearthkey.html

8. HOW AND WHY OF THE ECHN PROCESS Project NatureConnect 2008, How to Transform Destructive Thinking Into Constructive Relationships.
http://www.ecopsych.com/transformation.html

9. ATTRACTIVE SELF IDENTITY Project NatureConnect 2007 Whom Am I? Who or What is Your Natural Self? http://www.ecopsych.com/thesisquote6.html

10. DEALING WITH DUALITY Project NatureConnect 2005 Thinking and Learning With all Nine Legs

VALUE INDEX My degree of attraction to the information on this page:
1   2   3   4   5   6   7   8   9   10
   None   Moderate   Strong
IF IMPORTANT, WHY?

http://www.ecopsych.com/nineleg.html

11. FACTS AND CONSIDERATIONS Project NatureConnect 2007 Challenge: The Considerations of a Nature Expert http://www.ecopsych.com/mjcohen22.html

12. DESCRIBING THE ESSENCE Project NatureConnect 2007 Who, What or When is the acronym NNIAAL? http://www.ecopsych.com/earthstories101.html

13. SCIENTIFIC CONFIRMATION Higgs Boson Discovery http://news.nationalgeographic.com/news/2012/07/120704-god-particle-higgs-boson-new-cern-science/

14. VOCATIONAL PROSPECTS Project NatureConnect Adds a Nature-Love Practioner's Cooperative to its Natural Attraction Ecology Program. http://www.ecopsych.com/journalcooperative.html

15. DISCONNECTION REMEDY Project NatureConnect 2012 Ecozombie, Heal Thyself: The Universe, Earth and Humanity In Balance are Important http://www.ecopsych.com/journalproof.html

16. SELF EVIDENT FACTS Project NatureConnect Peak Fact: Whole Life Self Evidence in Action http://www.ecopsych.com/journalpeak.html

17. PNC AS ECOPSYCHOLOGY Doherty, T. J. 2010, Michael Cohen: Ecopsychology Interview Ecopsychology Journal, Vol 2 No.2. Mary Jane Liebert Publishing. http://www.ecopsych.com/ecopsychologyjournal.html

 18. NATURE CONNECTION OUTCOMES Project NatureConnect: Nature Connected Health and Wellness Research http://www.ecopsych.com/2004ecoheal.html

19. WHAT IS AN ECOZOMBIE? Project NatureConnect: Rehabilitate Ecozombie Sensitivities http://www.ecopsych.com/zombie.html

20. GUARANTEED ACCURACY Project NatureConnect: PNC Warranty: Singularity in Action http://www.ecopsych.com/journalwarranty.html

21. ONLINE EXPLORATION TRAIL Project NatureConnect: The Online Discovery Trail http://www.ecopsych.com/avatarpath.html

22. EDUCATING COUNSELING AND HEALING WITH NATURE Project NatureConnect: Homepage http://www.ecopsych.com

APPENDIX H
YOUR PERSONAL ACTIVITY PAGE RESPONSE FORM

NOTE: This page may also be downloaded at www.ecopsych.com/nhpresponse.docx and then copied and submitted by email or as an attachment to classmates or other friends (as may be required for online course responses).

Responses   (write your Validations)

Record   Notes, Reactions, Questions, Comments,
Increase Awareness Write responses to the following in the space provided in the NHP chapter you are reading or in a journal, or via the online form described above:

- How and what did you feel when you had this experience?
- The three most important things you learned from this experience?
- How would you feel about having the experience taken away from you?
- Did the activity enhance your sense of self-worth and your trustfulness of Nature/ your Other Body?
- Share your reactions with others and respond to what they share with you.
- Write one or two keywords that convey what important thing you learned from this assignment.
- Write one or more complete, single, short, power sentence "quotes" that convey a good contribution that this experience made toward improving your relationship with our Other Body.
- While your 5-leg mind sleeps, your 4-leg mind fills new paths of consciousness made by this activity. Note upon awakening whether any changes have occurred immediately, or in the next few days, with respect to the way you think, feel or act

Strengthening Activities: Match – Resonate – Appreciate – Trust – Celebrate   (see Appendix B)

Pass it on! You will increase your learning by 75% if you teach this information to another person.

Strengthen your ability to Validate through a leadership training workshop with Dr. Cohen and others on San Juan Island, Washington and elsewhere. By appointment 360.378.6313.

VALUE INDEX My degree of attraction to the information on this page:

1	2	3	4	5	6	7	8	9	10
	None				Moderate			Strong	

IF IMPORTANT, WHY?

ACTIVITY PAGE

RESPONSES write your Validations in the space provided below.

RECORD NOTES, Reactions, Questions, Comments, Drawings, Rubs, Samples

INCREASE AWARENESS Write responses to the activities found in Appendix H

DO POWER ACTIVITIES **Match – Resonate – Appreciate – Trust – Celebrate** *(see Appendix B).*

OPTION: arrange an onsite workshop with Dr. Cohen 1-360-378-6313

Text References are listed by number in Appendix G with online links.

LEARN MORE Master ECHN: online orientation course www.ecopsych.com/orient.html

PASS IT ON: Increase your expertise by 75%. Teach NHP to another person.

VALUE INDEX My degree of attraction to the information on this page:

1	2	3	4	5	6	7	8	9	10
	None				Moderate			Strong	

IF IMPORTANT, WHY?

www.ingramcontent.com/pod-product-compliance
Lightning Source LLC
Chambersburg PA
CBHW081435270326
41932CB00019B/3213